NOT IN

NOT IN MY NAME
A Compendium of Modern Hypocrisy

Julie Burchill and
Chas Newkey-Burden

Published by Virgin Books 2009

2 4 6 8 10 9 7 5 3 1

Copyright © Julie Burchill and Chas Newkey-Burden 2008

Julie Burchill and Chas Newkey-Burden have asserted their right under the
Copyright, Designs and Patents Act 1988 to be identified as the authors of this work

First published in Great Britain in 2008 by
Virgin Books
Random House
Thames Wharf Studios,
Rainville Road
London, W6 9HA

www.virginbooks.com
www.rbooks.co.uk

Addresses for companies within The Random House Group Limited can be
found at: www.randomhouse.co.uk/offices.htm

The Random House Group Limited Reg. No. 954009

A CIP catalogue record for this book is available from the British Library

ISBN 9780753516850

The Random House Group Limited supports The Forest Stewardship Council
[FSC], the leading international forest certification organisation. All our titles that
are printed on Greenpeace approved FSC certified paper carry the FSC logo.
Our paper procurement policy can be found at www.rbooks.co.uk/environment

Typeset by TW Typeseting, Plymouth, Devon
Printed in the UK by CPI Bookmarque, Croydon, CR0 4TD

CONTENTS

The Cost Of Fame

Hollywood Hypocrites; Guilty Pleasures; Hypocritical
Comedians; Reality Talent Shows, Sour-Faced Haters of;
Fame-Dissing Famous; Amy Winehouse Knockers;
Graffiti and the Guardianista; Posh Confessionals Vs
Common Kiss and Tells

Green Unpleasant Land

Cool Britannia; The Ex-Smoker; Mobiles and Emails;
Chav-Haters; Hypocrisy Towards the Homeless; The
Hypocrisy of Nostalgia; The Bullying Hypocrite; A Right
Royal Hypocrisy; Greens

Appendix

Hypocrites' Five Fave Footballers; The Hypocrites' Party
Manifesto; Hypocrites' Holidays; Top Five
Anti-Hypocrites; The Hypocrites' Ultimate Weekend

To Arik and Bibi

PREFACE

'War is an ugly thing, but not the ugliest of things; the decayed and degraded state of moral and patriotic feeling which thinks nothing is worth a war, is worse . . . A man who has nothing which he cares more about than he does about his personal safety is a miserable creature who has no chance at being free, unless made and kept so by the exertions of better men than himself.'

John Stuart Mill, *The Contest in America*

Hypocrisy, of course, is nothing new. Pots have been calling kettles black since the dawn of time. From the woes of the Pharisees in the Bible, through Geoffrey Chaucer's 'smyler with a knife under his cloak', to Tory MPs spouting family values while cheating on their wives, human history is dominated by double standards and duplicity. So what is this modern hypocrisy of which we speak?

It is the hypocrisy of those who should know better, and believe they do. The hypocrisy of the enlightened, of the hip, of those who – externally at least – hold admirable, humanitarian values, but behind closed doors, when push comes to shove, prove to be far darker beings. Nick Cohen examined the increasing darkness among this number in his brilliant book *What's Left?*. Having written for the *Guardian* and the *Big Issue* respectively, we too have come to realise that it is often those who shout loudest about what lovely people they are who have the worst secrets, and that the most wickedly hypocritical people often come under the liberal/left umbrella.

So those are our main suspects and, as far as a time-frame goes, when we talk of modern hypocrisy we will mean that which has taken place in the twenty-first century. Since the fireworks lit up the sky on New Year's Eve 1999, so much has changed. Many of the things that provoke modern hypocrisy – reality television, the concept of the 'chav', terrorism and environmentalism – either did not exist in the twentieth century, or did so in a form that is unrecognisable to us today. Thus is the twenty-first century becoming the heyday of the hypocrite, particularly since the 9/11 attacks, which were greeted with horrific and hypocritical responses by so many.

The modern hypocrite might deceive us with their duplicitous ways but we shouldn't take it personally for they deceive themselves, too. The writer André Gide said, 'The true hypocrite is the one who ceases to perceive his deception, the one who lies with sincerity.' By that yardstick, the modern hypocrite is the biggest, truest hypocrite of them all. We might not be fans of much of the manifesto of the right-wing, but we often find that those on the right are refreshingly honest when it comes to their own potential for hypocrisy.

In contrast, those on the modern liberal left increasingly believe that they are the most righteous of creatures and above criticism of any kind. It is far beyond their capability to accept that they might have any capacity for hypocrisy. Indeed, any suggestion that they might perhaps in some teeny-weeny way not be the most virtuous, perfect people alive is routinely received by them as if you've accused them of repeatedly punching a baby in the face. As such, they are prime candidates for the vice that has been described as 'prejudice with a halo'.

Rarely has there been a greater example of prejudice with a halo than in the modern anti-war movement. This book takes its name from the shameful, selfish slogan used by that movement: Not In My Name. The marchers' hypocrisy was stark: they used Britain's democracy and freedom of speech to angrily oppose the bringing of those very values to Iraqi people. They complained that Tony Blair wasn't listening to their views, while marching to keep in power a leader who tortured and murdered anyone who disagreed with his views. They moaned and whined at the slightest suggestion of their own civil liberties being curtailed as part of the fight against terrorism, but fell strangely silent when they heard about human rights abuses in some Muslim states. Then, a few years on, many of those marchers took to the streets again with banners reading, 'We're All Hezbollah Now', despite the fact that that group opposes every basic value most of the marchers hold dear.

Here's a thing though: it's actually not the likes of Hezbollah and their fellow Islamic extremists who are the hypocrites. Those who say women are filthy slaves, that gay men deserve to be executed and that democracy is undesirable are obviously extremely hateful but – fair's fair – not at all hypocritical. In fact, they're arguably the most straightforward and consistent people on the planet. The hypocrites are those who claim to support feminism and gay rights and yet align themselves with the vile movements that are the biggest opponents of those values, those who say they back democracy and yet consistently attack the Middle East's only true democracy – the state of Israel.

There's something about foreign affairs that brings out people's hypocrisies. The modern hypocrite loves a holiday – all that fakery is hard work, don'tcha know! – and as they flock to countries like Ireland, Cuba, Jamaica and Dubai they care little about the human rights records of those states. Indeed, the more we explored the topic, the more we began to suspect that many modern hypocrites do not overlook the savagery of their international idols, but are in some strange way turned on by it.

It's not just overseas where the double standards bite. At home, too, modern hypocrites rule the roost. Those who shout their opposition to racism from the rooftops are nevertheless delighted to pour the bitterest scorn on working-class people, or 'chav scum' as they so charmingly put it. Likewise, they'll wag their green fingers at those who take cheap package holidays while treading far bigger carbon footprints over the planet themselves. They'll give money to the homeless but then lord it over them, telling them what to spend it on. And anyone who has spent any time with an ex-smoker knows that hypocrisy is a way of life to them.

Yup, modern hypocrisy really does suck. In the comparatively good old days, hypocrisy meant Tory MPs who preached family values while banging their secretaries, or lefties espousing equality but pursuing a champagne lifestyle, or anti-drug firebrands who had smoked pot at university. It seemed serious and sickening at the time but now appears almost quaint and sweet when compared to its present-day counterpart. Modern hypocrisy straddles all walks of modern life from celebrity to politics, sexuality to sport, cycling to socialism, foreign affairs to extramarital affairs. From humungous hypocrisies to daily double standards, they're fine ones to talk and we've busted them all.

Exposing hypocrisy has always been a popular pastime for writers. Homer said, 'I detest that man, who hides one thing in the depths of his heart, and speaks forth another,' and here, in the twenty-first century, the fastest way to a newspaper editor's heart is to bring them a story that unmasks a hypocrite. As for us, we decided to write this book after finding that the common thread throughout our writing and our late-night chinwags was an intense dislike of hypocrisy, which has rightly been described as the only vice that cannot be forgiven.

A trend that props up a lot of modern hypocrisy is the shame that is increasingly attached to the idea of changing your mind. Should a politician or public figure dare to alter their opinion on any matter, they're knocked off their feet by a succession of 'U-Turn Shame' headlines. Since when did having a mind that is open to change become something to be ashamed of? Both of us have previously held different views on some of the subjects that follow. Indeed, as we repeatedly found while writing this book, the conflicts and perils of the twenty-first century have seen many of us take up alliances that would have seemed unimaginable in the past. We would argue, however, that, though we have sometimes changed side, the philosophy behind our stances has remained largely consistent.

You know, it's just not safe to go out on the streets any more. Everywhere you turn you are forced to dodge stones being flung from glass houses, or protect your ears from the deafening din of people saying, 'Do as I say, not as I do,' and all this is going on amid the rising, rotten stench of hypocrisy that pollutes the very air we breathe. So stay at home, put your feet up and join us as we unmask the ghastly creature that is the modern hypocrite.

Julie Burchill and Chas Newkey-Burden, 2008

FUN AND GAMES

Fat-Girl Feminists; Strong Women; Nearly Men, or 'gay-friendly' homophobes; The White Hip-Hop Fan; 'Straight' Women Who Don't Like Men; Old Feminists Who Slag Off Young Women For Doing the Same Sort of Stuff They Did When They Were Young; Up the Bum; Gay Hypocrisy; Masturbation; The Hypocritical Game; The Ageism of the Gay Man; Cyclists; Ugly Sexist Men

FAT-GIRL FEMINISTS
Julie Burchill

I'm a very off-message type of fat girl: one who gladly – gluttonously, even! – admits that at one point she reached the mighty dress size of 22 solely through lack of discipline and love of pleasure. And who, it must be said, tends to despise people – except those with actual medical conditions – who pretend that it is often otherwise.

Gluttony and idleness are two of life's great joys, but they are neither honourable nor political – no more than their opposite values, dieting and exercise. And the people – largely women – who claim otherwise are literally big fat hypocrites, insisting as they do that practising gluttony and idleness makes you 'better' and less shallow than the people who avoid them.

'Big women' do themselves no favours when they attempt to reposition themselves as the Righteous Fat. The Righteous Thin are bad enough with all that running around and sweating and somehow believing that it means anything more than being thin, such as achieving something or living for ever. But the Righteous Fat (unlike the Righteous Thin, who do at least put themselves out in order to achieve their goal) are hypocrites to boot. They want to have their cake, eat it and then say, 'Yes – I'm a REAL person!' As though gluttony and idleness make one more 'real'!

These Lard Legionnaires frequently lay claim not just to righteousness by dint of their obesity, but also to feminism, for some reason. And then, this done, they flex their feminist muscle – flab, rather – by picking on their skinny sisters; a heavyweight–flyweight mob-handed cat fight, for the delight of drooling male onlookers! Now that's hypocrisy and a half.

A lethal combination of Fat Righteousness and Fat Feminism led to an awful epidemic some years back of overweight media broads who ceaselessly boasted to anyone who'd listen about what brilliant sex lives they had. I was among the culprits, to be fair. But – here's the rub – my bragging was purely personal; not once did I say that my size had anything to do with my sex life. Others, on the other hand, claimed that fat women had more and better sex than thin women.

I remember thinking how incredibly bitchy and bigoted this was, but most of all how singularly unfeminist; to imply that the amount of sex a woman has somehow validates her as a human being.

And there it is again, you see – the hollow ring of Fat-Girl Feminism, the bleating behind the bluster and the bellies: 'Why do men like those skinny bitches more than meeee?' But surely one of the advantages of being a feminist is that one doesn't give a stuff about trivia such as whether one's particular body shape is in favour – with men! – or not.

So I declined to join in this orgy of denial for the simple reason that I found/find it as ludicrous for women to be 'proud' of being fat as I do for women to be 'proud' of being thin. One can be rightly proud of one's work, or of being kind, or any number of achievements or personal qualities. But to be proud of one's BMI, be it high or low, seems to me truly tragic.

Still, despite all this, I've actually got these particular modern hypocrites to thank for my long hard journey back from the Empire Of Elasticated Waists. Their mantra of 'Thin women = neurotic and sexless; fat women = fun-fun-fun' finally gave me the wake-up call every fat bird needs – the fervent desire never, ever to be like them, be it in body or soul. For beauty is only skin deep, but ugliness cuts to the bone.

In an interesting updating of the folly of Fat-Girl Feminism – but this time with a further hypocritical hint of Caring Capitalism – a couple of years back Dove, the touchy-feely toiletries brand owned by the huge international Unilever corporation, launched its Campaign For Real Beauty. Jaded old cynic that I am, I couldn't help thinking of that old line by the French diplomat and writer Jean Giraudoux, 'The secret of success is sincerity. Once you can fake that you've got it made.'

Dove have been peddling soap, deodorant, shampoo and 'body-firming' cream over here since the 1990s; more than seven million women a week use Dove products in the UK alone. As toiletries go, they're fine; I used to use them occasionally myself. But toiletries is ALL they are!

Where does one start to describe what is so creepy about this 'campaign'? Let alone the related Dove Self-Esteem Fund, which aims to challenge conventional ideals of beauty and encourage every female to feel 'positive' about her appearance:

It's time to shake up self-esteem! And to give body image a boost. Every day we are bombarded by hundreds – if not thousands – of airbrushed images of 'beauty' . . . images with the power to affect how we see our bodies and ourselves. But who defines these beauty standards? How can we turn the tide of such beauty pressures and encourage young girls and women everywhere to embrace a more positive body image? We believe it's time to find the answers . . . with your help!

I'll do my best! Well, for a start, would it be churlish to point out that a good number of these 'airbrushed images of beauty' with which we are 'bombarded' every day come at us in commercials for such brands as Impulse fragrances, Lux soap, Pond's cold cream, Sunsilk shampoo and Sure deodorant? All of which just happen to be owned by the Fat Girl's Friend – Unilever!

Not that I personally ever feel 'bombarded' by images of attractive people; on the contrary, I enjoy them without feeling threatened by them, probably because I value myself for other attributes apart from my looks. Far more offensive to me – though, come to think of it, even these leave me sneering rather than shrieking – are the numerous daily images which suggest that women can achieve multiple orgasms simply by using the correct household cleansing agents – thank you Persil, Surf, Cif and Comfort, all courtesy of Unilever.

Another answer I'd be happy to help Dove with is that there actually seems to be something about their specific products that implies (far more than the 'airbrushed beauty' brigade) that there is something inherently wrong with women's bodies. For instance, their insistence on making their antiperspirant one quarter moisturising lotion – not only are women being told that they smell, but that their armpits resemble minging old bits of sandpaper! How the heck this insinuation helps to improve female self-esteem I have no idea – maybe Dove could help me find the answer.

And to come full circle right back to the matter of FGF with which I began this essayette, perhaps the most irritating thing about the Dove Do-Gooders is their repeated insistence that REAL WOMEN HAVE REAL CURVES. It's irritating – for the same reason as the old Marks & Spencer television commercial with that size 16 sort running naked up a hill yelling, 'I'M NORMAL!' – because it smacks not of the genuine self-esteem that comes only from an individual's respect for themselves, regardless of what the world thinks of them, but of some skanky little ad-man smarming, 'Now let's squeeze some money out of the fat girls – they're always suckers for a bit of flattery!' It's the liberal media equivalent of a Pull-A-Pig contest.

Paradoxically, in its cack-handed attempt to be inclusive, the Dove propaganda actually ends up as exclusive as any image of airbrushed perfection – which at least all semi-sentient people KNOW is a con as photographs of the real-life models looking nothing like their doctored ad campaigns frequently show. But 'Real women have real curves' – what an elitist, spiteful, thoughtless statement, while all the time claiming to be interested in elevating female self-esteem! What about flat-chested women? What about women who have had mastectomies!

The fact is that a woman with true self-esteem doesn't give two hoots about something as time-consuming and approval-seeking as changing perceptions of what is beautiful in general and of herself in particular. As men's have always done, a real woman's very presence declares, 'This is me – take it or leave it, for your opinion is of no consequence to me!' There may have been a time when this wasn't reasonable or wise behaviour – when we depended upon men for financial upkeep – but it certainly is now, unless one is an actress, a model or a prostitute.

So, to sum up, real women certainly don't waste their one and only life on earth wheedling, 'Ooo, ooo, I may not be a size zero but I'm beautiful too; love me, pleeease!' as the Dovettes do – that's the OPPOSITE of self-esteem and, even more so, of feminism. Real women don't necessarily have curves – some chicks have tiny tits and useless arses, but they're as real as the rest of us. Real women aren't in the least threatened by or hostile to thin women; on the contrary, they can easily enjoy their otherworldly, differently abled contribution to our culture, and see them first and foremost as our sisters under the skin. Even if there is a lot less of it.

Last but not least, real women don't sell their souls for advertising's scummy shilling – only Satan's little helpers do that. Eat that, Fat-Girl Feminists!

STRONG WOMEN
Julie Burchill

'STRONG LOOKS FOR STRONG WOMEN!' ran a 2007 AOL screamer, trailing the new-season fashions. 'THINK BIG, BE BOLD – AND LET THE CLOTHES DO THE TALKING THIS AUTUMN!' The Strong Woman has always been a hypocrite's poster-girl pin-up. There are two basic versions of her, and each one displays a different face of duplicity.

There's the Self-Proclaimed Strong Woman – as in 'Men are intimidated by me because I'm a Strong Woman; they just can't handle me!' Yep, whenever some sleb serial spinster – or even one's ex-best friend, for this is a cliché that has really caught on among bunny boilers of all social classes – wants to do a bit of damage limitation over the indignity of being dumped by her latest bored boulevardier, at some point she'll come out with this line. Funny, that; in my experience, any man worthy of the name is only too happy to have a Her Indoors who can lighten his load in more ways than one, rather than a simpering Baby Jane manqué who needs her hand held to open an envelope. Or a clingy hysteric who sincerely believes that 'You Oughta Know' by Alanis Morissette – the Canadian who, to my ears at least, sounds like a car! – is an anthem for Strong Women everywhere. D'oh! – it's all about having a nervous breakdown just because some clown's dumped you – what's strong about that?!

This mode of hostile dependency, fuelled by narcissistic self-loathing – 'You dumped me like a dog, but I'm too good for you!' – has spawned quite a selection of sad little artefacts, from pop songs by the likes of Avril Lavigne, Beyoncé and Jennifer Lopez to magazine adverts such as 'THIS IS MY MEETING THE EX AND I WANT HIM TO KNOW WHAT HE'S MISSING COLLECTION' (Oli clothing) and 'YOU KNOW WHAT, MARK? YOU WERE RIGHT. I AM TOO GOOD FOR YOU' (Charles Worthington).

Some 'strong women' have gone even further and proclaimed themselves to be Strong Black Women. Whereas a self-proclaimed Strong (White) Woman is an aforementioned weak ninny, an other-defined Strong Black Woman actually is genuinely tough; she can deal with six things before breakfast that would have the rest of us banging on the door of the Laughing Academy. BUT . . . her ability to cope gets her no real respect beyond lip service; thus, 'She's a Strong Black Woman', while sounding on the surface respectful, actually means, 'So I can do what I like to her!' The great black feminist writer Michele Wallace recalled watching a 1970s TV documentary about a horrifically poor black woman with half a dozen children, all of them living in rat-infested squalor in some wretched hovel; the black radical man watching it with her said admiringly, 'That's one strong sister!' No: that's a punching bag, a dumping ground, a person who has had their identity stolen from them by a succession of men who relied on her to take it, and stay 'strong'. Since then gangsta has replaced pantha, and women who should know better have embraced this destructive myth – albeit more to keep the bling on their fingers than the roof over their head.

As I said, both types of Strong Women are a seat-sniffing hypocrite's wet dream: the white model pronounces herself strong while being weak, and the black version is lauded as strong by a man who treats her like she's seven sorts of wimp. But at least the other-defined Strong Black Woman is a tragedy, and has the dignity of that condition, while the self-proclaimed Strong (White) Woman is never more or less than a downright clown.

It's a topsy-turvy world, all right. Bleat, whine and endlessly pick at your wounds – self-inflicted, imaginary or otherwise – and/or let men take advantage of you, and you have every chance of passing as a Strong Woman. But smile, shrug and say, 'Onwards and upwards!' and you'll be dismissed as 'in denial', and thus a suitable case for treatment. In the past, women had to pretend to be stupid to be deemed acceptable to society; frequently these days they must pretend to be complex, traumatised 'survivors'. In the light of this sexist, miserabilist, hypocritical orthodoxy, surely clear-eyed, hard-hearted happiness is the most maddeningly subversive weapon a modern girl can wield!

And another thing . . .

Strong Woman, meet Working Girl – you've got loads in common! Mostly that you both seem to believe, somewhat hypocritically and against all the evidence, that you are somehow more worthy of the name you give yourself than are the numerous other women who don't swank around laying claim to it, but are nevertheless far more worthy of it.

I adore my prostitute friends, but when I hear them use the phrases 'working girl', 'Did/does she work?' or 'Is she working?' I feel my eyes actually cross in contempt. For they speak not of the sisterhood of toil in all its various bravery, stoicism and intelligence, but solely of that part of it that decided at a young age that taking it in the face from various dirty old men was a price worth paying in order to sleep late, take drugs and drink shorts with sleazeballs when other women are slogging home from the nine to five.

And before any Guardianista has the PC ab-dabs here, OBVIOUSLY – duh! – I'm not talking about some poor exploited and trafficked Eastern European chick who is only being trafficked and exploited in the first place because people like you think it's really, like, fascist not to let in every last Albanian pimp who says it's his human right to be here. No, I'm talking about your average home-grown domestic prossie, who made a deliberate decision somewhere along the line that skiving on her knees was better than working on her feet.

Fair enough – but, whatever the rights and wrongs of the issue, and however nice individual prostitutes may be as people, to imply that other women – nurses, teachers, cleaners – don't work is downright insulting, not to mention hypocritical. Call me a common chav – go on, you know you want to! – but, where I come from, lying on one's back for a living is considered the lazy cow option rather than the workaholic one.

NEARLY MEN, OR 'GAY-FRIENDLY' HOMOPHOBES

Chas Newkey-Burden

If there's one type of person who has got the art of contradicting fine words with foul deeds down to a tee, then that person is the Nearly Man. These duplicitous dudes stand out as particularly odious, even in the packed roll-call of hypocrisy that is modern life. Their double standards are particularly striking when it comes to their attitudes to women and gay men, towards whom these guys are barely less savage than the misogynists and homophobes of yesteryear, but with the veneer of being right-on.

In my experience, just as those who we gay people fear will hate us can actually be rather sweet in their own way, it is also often those who shout loudest about their love for us who can be the most offensive and downright terrifying in their attitudes. I've met plenty of the latter, hypocritical category in the land of the media: white, middle-class, heterosexual, thirty-something men who read the *Guardian*, profess to be humanitarian and appear – to all intents and purposes – thoroughly decent blokes. Just the sort of person gay men should get along with, you might say.

Or not. In my experience, it is the middle-class goody-goody straight boys who are the most hung up about gay people and consequently most spiteful towards us, albeit in a more subtle and sly way.

Most people refer to these guys as 'New Men', but I prefer to call them 'Nearly Men'. Theirs is a peculiarly modern hypocrisy: they start from the premise that 'I'm not homophobic' and, of course, once they have established that, they can say anything they like to gay people; if you dare complain, they'll paint you as the troublemaker and remind you, with a patronising smile, 'But I'm not homophobic. I'm with you guys, remember?' They're not with us at all, of course. I've had far more hurtful comments thrown at me from Nearly Men than any other type of person, including the Jack-the-lad types I worked with in football.

Nearly Men's problems with gay men actually originate from their increasingly troubled relationship with the fairer sex. They've lost sight of the fact that their dealings with women do not have to be one of two extremes – either bossing them about like bastards or grovelling behind them like terrified, shivering eunuchs. Of course, there is a whole happy world between these two extremes and it's called respect and chivalry. But Nearly Men can't seem to get that right, so more and more of them become a parody of the henpecked husband and end up full of liberal resentment because they feel like they've been castrated. Then, as they become fathers and their midriffs expand, the male-pattern baldness kicks in and their wives keep making elaborate excuses at bedtime – or the singletons among them realise they cannot pull for love nor money – their resentment of women builds and builds.

Accordingly, they begin to look on gay men with resentment. With increasing bewilderment, too! The Nearly Men were taught in their liberal schooling that they have to be nice to the gays. But, in return, they held out hope for two things. One, they expected that we would be good little gays who would remain forever grateful to them for their support and respect. Two, they also expected that our lives would become more and more tragic, while their lives became more and more brilliant. Instead, they can't help feeling that their lives are becoming more and more banal and so they eye with increasing envy our lives, which they see as one long party with sex on tap and minimal responsibility.

The terrible truth, though, is that some of these Nearly Men have far more colourful sex lives than a lot of gays. Many a time I have sat with them in the pub and they've expressed horror at the fact that so many gays have arrangements such as open relationships and that sex is so readily available to gay men. 'I dunno how you guys can live like that,' they snarl. But, by the time we are staggering around outside the kebab shop at closing time, their hypocrisy once again becomes clear as they confess all to me about their fruity extramarital shags behind the wife's back. Each occurrence just a 'one-off', of course! I've had more than a few colourful moments in my life, but I'm like a chastity-vowed monk when compared to some of the supposedly goody-goody men I've gone drinking with. Not that I'm going prudish on them, of course. I just wish they'd stop finger-wagging at others in public while shagging left, right and centre in private! They're like the twenty-first-century, liberal equivalent of all those humping hypocrites John Major had in his Cabinet in the 1990s.

Let's not be too harsh, though, because, thankfully, for every Nearly Man there is a real man, who can at least speak truthfully. I'll take them over a Nearly Man any day of the week. So give me those lads I worked with in football who called me 'gay boy', but did so to my face, and also promised they'd beat up anyone who ever genuinely upset me. Give me the Muslim friend who told me that, according to his book, what I do is a sin, and then, when I told him his 'book' meant nothing to me, laughed and said, 'Phew. Glad we've got all that out of the way.' Give me the vicar who, at a particularly churchy, conservative wedding I attended with my boyfriend, stepped up to the disco decks and put on 'YMCA' by the Village People and gave me and my boy the thumbs up in a cringeworthy but well-meant gesture of welcome.

Give me pretty much anyone, in fact, ahead of the confused, castrated Nearly Man with his subtle, patronising sneering attitude to gay men and women. It's interesting that people still talk about 'the closet' because that concept can now be just as easily applied to homophobes as it can to gay men. Just because homophobia has become unfashionable, that doesn't mean it's gone away. The Nearly Man is just as down on gays as the old-fashioned men he believes he is so much more enlightened than. However, at least in the olden days they were honest about their feelings!

As for the Nearly Man, however much he pretends not to be, he's a deluded hypocrite if he thinks he is particularly enlightened in his dealings with women or if he 'accepts' gay men. His is a homophobia and misogyny with a copy of the *Guardian* rolled up under its arm. Away with him. I don't care whether his problem is that he regrets getting buggered at public school, or regrets not getting buggered at public school – his kind of enlightenment and acceptance I can do without.

THE WHITE HIP-HOP FAN
Chas Newkey-Burden

The soundtrack to the lives of many Nearly Men is hip hop, so let's take a look at their relationship with this genre. To be honest, I've never liked the music myself, but I'll admit I've never really given it a chance. Call me an old reactionary, but the moment I spotted all that rampant misogyny, homo-phobia and anti-Semitism dragging its knuckles over the hill, I decided my record collection could get by without it. All the same, plenty of Nearly Men have tried to inform me of the genre's many merits. They are always full of enthusiasm about how wonderful and clever the lyrics are, if only I would sit and actually listen to them. It's all about the lyrics!

So I listen to the lyrics and point out that they so often aggressively diss women and gays. These studious observers and admirers of hip-hop lyrics then hold their hands up with shock, 'Really? I had no idea the song had that message!' So do they really have no idea that the lyrics written by a gaggle of rap artists are full of homophobic drivel? Have all these lyrics passed them by?

Of course, for every moment of homophobia in rap there are many hours of misogyny. Women are routinely described as 'bitches' and 'hoes' by the rappers who glorify pimp culture. The videos that accompany all this nonsense are often full of negative images of black women. These white hip-hop fans claim to be the pinnacles of anti-racism, yet their favourite artists' videos routinely disrespect and dehumanise black women to an extent that any daft old racist would find hard to better.

If I, who never watches or listens to hip-hop TV and radio stations, have noticed all this, could it really have escaped the attention of the white hip-hop fan? Or could it be that, far from being ignorant of all this bigotry, it is actually the homophobia and misogyny of hip hop that secretly appeals to these guys, giving them a chance to be just as nasty to women and gays as their fathers' generation was, but with a veneer of respectability?

There's no denying that being gay has its hassles, but I must be honest and declare that it also has many benefits, and a major one of these is asking hypocritical Nearly Men, who claim to be gay-friendly, why exactly it is that they so passionately idolise rappers who call for brutality and violence against gays on a regular basis. Watching them struggle for some sort of clarity within their relativist, liberal consciences – 'Ooh, do I side with the gays or side with the blacks? It's so hard! I want my mummy!' – is a treat I find increasingly difficult to resist. I know I'm naughty but, really, it's so funny to watch, and they started it!

Their flustered, liberal soul-searching normally concludes with them muttering something about freedom of speech. So, to test their commitment to freedom of speech, I've often asked them how they'd feel if, say, a white heavy-metal outfit wrote a song calling for black men to be murdered. Would they want that on prime-time television and radio? At this point, they normally sulk for a while and then take me to one side and say, 'I accept that some rappers might occasionally say some nasty things about gay people but, if you knew anything about hip hop, you'd know such people are very few and far between.'

I then simply remind them that it was hip-hop royalty Kanye West who admitted, 'Everyone in hip hop discriminates against gays.' Then they storm off, presumably to have a wank over their Puff Daddy posters. (And how gay is the name

Puff Daddy, incidentally? It could be the name of a chat room on Gaydar.co.uk or, at the very least, the title of some sort of murky gay porn flick. Not that I'd know about either of those worlds, mind.) Of course, not all hip hop is homophobic, but West's quote surely proves that we're not talking about a small problem here.

To be fair, it's not just men who come out with this drivel; women have occasionally been known to do it, too. In her *Guardian* column, the normally great Zoe Williams wrote, 'If you look at the seminal black artists at the start of hip hop, Public Enemy and Niggaz With Attitude, you won't actually find much homophobia.' Not much homophobia? She doesn't enlighten us as to just how much would be acceptable, nor how much, say, racism would be acceptable to her and her *Guardian* chums if a white skinhead band came out with it.

But it's nearly always the white boys – it is estimated that four out of five rap albums are bought by such creatures – who are so quick to defend rap's worst excesses. In their blind support for woman-hating, gay-bashing rappers, the Nearly Men presumably believe that they're engaging in a sort of liberal trade-off: they might be offending one minority group (gays), but at least they're not offending another (black people). Their trade-off doesn't work, though, because, by implication, they are being most offensive to black people. Their argument boils down to this: black men must be forgiven for homophobia and misogyny because the brutes know no better.

Of course, the truth is that homophobia is no more acceptable in a black rap artist than it is in a white Roman Catholic or a gang of far-right skinheads. To suggest otherwise really is racist. It is interesting and apt, therefore, that of all the rap and reggae fans I've argued the toss with over homophobic lyrics, the only people I've ever ended up seeing eye to eye with on the topic are non-white rap fans.

'STRAIGHT' WOMEN WHO DON'T LIKE MEN
Julie Burchill

Whenever I see my homosexualist friends, I know that we're going to talk about everything from why 'trailer trash' is such a disgusting para-racist term to why the Monkees were so much better than Bob Dylan, the Beatles and the Rolling Stones put together. But one thing we're NOT going to talk about is how AWFUL men are. Because obviously, we don't think so. If we did, we wouldn't fall in love with them, and we wouldn't sleep with them; in short, I'd be gay and they'd be straight.

This being the case, I declare myself mystified by the popularity of TV shows such as *Queer Eye For The Straight Guy* and *Fairy Godfathers* in which gay men and – allegedly – 'straight' women conspire to turn men into sweet-smelling, flower-arranging, quiche-cooking castrates. For a start, it's incredibly hypocritical of gay men to pretend that they find unreconstructed masculinity unacceptable; turn to the back of any queer magazine and check out the sex fantasy lines! There are any number of GET GANG-BANGED BY A SKINHEAD SQUADDIE AND HIS SIX STRAIGHT MATES! scenarios, but you will search in vain for GET TAKEN TO THE IDEAL HOME EXHIBITION BY A MILD-MANNERED MANICURIST! storylines. No, generally speaking, nice gay men like rough boys, the 'straighter' the better; like Groucho Marx not wanting to join any club that would accept him as a member, a significant number of them wouldn't dream of dating anyone 'queeny'. Yet there they are on reality TV, taking the sort of straight lads they fantasise about and turning them from Arthur (Mullard) into Martha (Stewart).

But I'm not actually blaming the gay men involved in these shows for these flaky make-overs; after all, they have no loyalty towards the 'unacceptable' young men who they are called to sprinkle their fairy dust upon. What puzzles me is why the women who offer up their men as suitable cases for transformation feel the way they do about them – and why they prefer them once they have been stripped of their 'old-fashioned' masculine foibles, and re-created as mincing, moisturised, thoroughly modern milksops.

To paraphrase Freud, what do women like? And what do they like it more than? We've all heard about that creepy survey in which, appropriately, the men's heart rate went up and their pupils dilated when they were shown photographs of naked women, but with the women participants, the same physical reaction took place not when they were shown photos of naked men, but of naked babies! You're meant to think that's a lovely, cuddly fact, proving how 'nurturing' women are compared to sex-mad men, but frankly I find it tragic. And can we imagine the fuss if the MEN had reacted to naked babies that way!

So a lot of women prefer naked babies to naked men, for whatever reason; then there are those surveys claiming that most broads prefer shopping to sex, and chocolate to sex, and even a good night's sleep to sex when they're staying in hotels, according to a survey on the hotel booking and review website skoosh.com. Pretty soon there will be a survey showing that women prefer shaving their legs to sex, the way things are going. Put all this together and you'd be forgiven for coming to the conclusion that women don't really like sex much at all, relatively. Sex with men, that is. But perhaps that's because they yearn for sex of a different sort.

Exactly how gay are girls today? On one hand you can't dip a toe into the mass media without getting an eyeful of girl-on-girl action, while I myself have quite often had to dispatch drunken, drooling 'straight' women out into the night for wrongly assuming that I was up for a bit of 'experimentation' just because I fell in love with a girl, for six months, more than a decade ago. 'If you want to experiment, go and get yourself a test tube and a Bunsen burner!' is usually my final indignant word on the matter.

But how much did the likes of Madge snogging Brit reflect more on the increasing porno-isation of society than the new sexual confidence of women? In one way, thespian-lesbianism can be seen as just another flavour of taste-thrill laid on by women desperate to get/keep men, like saucy undies and 'sharing' dirty videos. In some ways, these days, it seems that one of the most feminist, rebellious things a woman could say would be, 'I don't fancy women,' as this would mark her out as someone not at all interested in titillating men. Ten years ago a man could divorce his wife for sleeping with a woman, whereas now, in some circles, he could probably divorce her if she didn't: 'It was unreasonable behaviour, M'Lud – depriving me of a nice bit of girl-on-girl!'

And yet, and yet – is it really so easy to routinely snog a species that you have no real interest in? At the risk of revealing myself to be an absolute ocean-going perve, I often during my sordid youth used to try to persuade my boyfriend du jour to sleep with his cutest friend so I could watch, and not one of them was up for it, the spoilsports.

There's got to be a spark there to start with, and in my opinion, much of play-lesbianism is actually a double-bluff, being there apparently to do nothing more than render one an even more agreeable playmate to men, but actually revealing a deep and constant strain of female distaste for the male genitalia which goes far deeper than copying desperate-for-attention pop-tarts.

OLD FEMINISTS WHO SLAG OFF YOUNG WOMEN FOR DOING THE SAME SORT OF STUFF THEY DID WHEN THEY WERE YOUNG

Julie Burchill

Oh, the sheer relief of growing old! To lose one's pesky good looks, to cease being chained to a tiny pink madman with a mind of its own – one's genitalia – and to concentrate instead on the real stuff of life: gout, grey hair, is it OK to ride one's mobility scooter on the pavement while off one's face on class-A drugs – that sort of thing. Oh, the joy of finally leaving childish things behind!

And becoming an old feminist, in particular, is surely something to look forward to. Now we'll really get to prove that character matters more than beauty, that the menopause is not synonymous with mental collapse. And, most of all, we'll be able to set a grand example to young women – our little sisters who, at the height of their beauty and ability, are often insecure and unsure of themselves, as we once were before we lost our looks and gained our selves. We can mentor them, even, thus enhancing our own credibility and reputation, do good by doing good, and into the bargain seriously stick the finger up to the multitudes of meat-brained men who love to stick a smirking spoke in the feminist ideal by pointing out that women have been too busy catfighting among themselves since the dawn of time ever to pose any threat to patriarchy.

I would maintain that most older feminists, like myself, totally live up to this. But there are a few very visible, very noisy ones who do their very best to let the side down time and time again. Once militantly opposed to everything the *Daily Mail* stood for – best summed up as 'SOMEWHERE A WOMAN IS HAVING FUN AND IT MUST BE STOPPED!' – they can now frequently be found taking its sullied shilling in return for rants entitled, 'WHY LADETTES/BIG BROTHER GIRLS/WAGS/ANY WOMAN UNDER THE AGE OF SIXTY BETRAYS EVERYTHING WE FEMINISTS BELIEVED IN'. Their hypocrisy is twofold: not only do they scold young women for doing things they did loads of in their youth – getting drunk, having sex, showing their tits – but they also draw the conclusion that this makes said young women anti-feminist, unsisterly and rude, while spitting abuse at them all the while – pot, kettle, black! And these are the same women who used to pick on Mrs Thatcher for being a bad feminist just because she didn't bend over backwards to promote her fellow females . . .

It's a lovely thing that in recent years this country's senior citizens have begun to behave irresponsibly, spending the money that their grasping, parasitical middle-aged offspring imagined was coming straight to them on fuchsia leisurewear and fjord cruises. It's a cool thing to be enjoying your second childhood at an age when the people whose bums you once wiped are planning to put you out to grass in a granny flat. But does such delightful regression really have to include the worst bits of being childish? That is, the bullying and cattiness of the schoolyard?

Speaking as an Old Feminist myself, I strongly feel that it is the behaviour of broads old enough to know better. And reluctantly – but not too reluctantly, heh heh! – I come to the conclusion that sheer, old-fashioned envy is the root of such pseudo-superior spite; when the nipples go south, the nose goes north. And it is such behaviour – not a few young chicks getting their tits out for the *Sun* – that really does the dirty on feminism. While conveniently identifying one as a rabid hypocrite, of course!

And another thing . . .

Speaking of the *Daily Mail*, were we truly to do justice to the amount of hypocrisy that lies within that paper's pages, we'd be here all year. However, their casino campaign cannot go without mention. Days after it boasted of its 'Very Moral Victory' against the introduction of Las Vegas-style casinos in the UK, it was pointed out that the *Daily Mail*'s own online gambling site failed to adhere to industry guidelines and used young people to promote its games. The website quickly disappeared, but the stench of hypocrisy remains.

UP THE BUM
Julie Burchill

Sex is a funny old business. And, as is often the case in the happy world of heterosexuality, the sexes don't even seem to agree on what it is. Women seem to believe sex should be about sharing, talking, communication, lighting one hundred scented candles, taking an hour-long aromatherapy bath, being given a two-hour-long massage with oil that smells like someone sicked up a whole box of Milk Tray at once, kissing, cuddling, stroking . . . and that other thing, you know, that's really rude and boring. And then more cuddling. Basically, a cross between a trip to Disneyland and a play date with Barbie. (What excuse did women use for not having sex before 'We've run out of scented candles'?)

Men seem to believe sex should be about sex, the dirty swine.

The final insult to a man's pride and a woman's intelligence is when some broad who says she's in love with you turns down a perfectly good offer of a quick bout of sodomy – free of charge – because 'I don't like anything up there.' And then goes off to pay a perfect stranger a small fortune for colonic irrigation! Now that's a hypocrite and a half, with bells on!

GAY HYPOCRISY
Chas Newkey-Burden

A key character trait of the hypocrite is an ability to dish it out but none at all to take it back. How wonderfully ironic it is, then, that there is so much hypocrisy in gay land – because gay men, of all people, should be very good at giving and taking. If only it were true! The horrible reality is that citing 'what our people have been put through' as a catch-all excuse – in reality a mere stroll in the park compared to so many other people's experiences of hardship – gay men have become increasingly self-righteous and, as we've seen throughout these pages, self-righteousness is the civil partner of hypocrisy.

One of the gay hypocrite's favourite hobbies is to desperately ascribe homosexuality to the behaviour of heterosexual men. 'Interesting, that's very homoerotic,' they whisper knowingly when they see straight men showing even the mildest forms of physical affection to one another. Note here that straight men are in a no-win situation: if they won't hug one another then they are 'uptight hetero homophobes' but, if they do, then apparently 'they must be gay'.

Likewise, whenever an attractive straight male celebrity crops up in conversation, the gay hypocrite will shriek, 'Straight? Oh, come off it! She's not kidding anyone!' (How interesting that when they want to put a man down, they call him 'she'.) Then there's that horribly embarrassing little joke so beloved of the gay desperado: 'What's the difference between a straight man and a gay man? About ten pints of lager.'

You wish! The sheer desperation of this joke speaks for itself, so let's examine the hypocrisy of it instead. For just you try suggesting to these wise-gays that, were it true that all straight men have a gay side, then surely all gay men must have a straight side – and wait for the howls of horror and dissent. Full of stories of friends or relatives who have told them 'Maybe it's just a phase you're going through,' these gays refuse to accept that anyone else understands them or their sexuality at all. The whole 'you don't understand me' thing is always tiresome, but especially so when it comes from the mouths of people who insist they have a special insight into everyone else's sexuality.

And anyway, in your dreams, lads! The desperation of this dream is also laid bare when the gay hypocrite attempts to frighten and get one up on his female friends by saying, 'You wanna watch it, girls, because gay men know what your boyfriends really want in bed.' Oh dear. Gay pride? I don't think I've ever felt so embarrassed.

MASTURBATION
Julie Burchill

You always hear that there's a 'double standard' when it comes to sex. A male, so the line goes, is free to do as he pleases sexually and, the more he does it, the more he'll be admired by men and desired by women. Whereas a woman who does the same is despised by all.

But there's an interesting exception here. And it's no less hypocritical than the old 'me stud, you slut' duplicity. You could call it Hands-On Hypocrisy.

That exception is masturbation. Yep – when it comes to our shouty old mate Self Abuse, contemporary public opinion does a drastic about-face. A man who masturbates is inadequate, lonely, scared of women – the 'sad tosser' of legend, in fact. He can't get a girlfriend! BUT a woman who masturbates is empowered, autonomous, freed from male oppression. She doesn't WANT or NEED a boyfriend!

It gets better. A man who buys a sex doll or – even more so! – a replica of female genitalia is not just sad, but a bona fide weirdo. BUT a woman who buys vibrators, dildos and the like is somehow a superior being to those of her sisters who rely on a boring old living, breathing playmate for kicks.

It gets worse. Whereas men will good-naturedly make do with any old cheap'n'cheerful pocket-pussy, women are prepared to pay a fortune for their disembodied genital substitutes. A glass dildo from Coco de Mer costs one thousand pounds; imagine how odd you'd have to be to spend that much on a pretend cock that you could snap in half if you got carried away! Not to mention picking out the splinters afterwards.

Just why is the urban myth of the man who allegedly had sex with a vacuum cleaner and had to go to A&E to get himself disengaged from it so contemptuously hilarious, while the woman who spends a cool thou on a glass cock is supposed to be some sort of sorted, post-feminist heroine? At least if it was a Henry Hoover it'd have a cute little smiling face on it and bear at least a passing resemblance to a human being. But how do you factor a glass cock into your fantasies? Who's your dream date – the Invisible Man?

As for those types who own vibrators disguised as bath ducks, rabbits and various other children's toys – you do the maths, and, when you've done it, call 999! Astoundingly, it's meant to be a proper cute hoot – yet, if a man has sex with a toy animal, everyone thinks he's some sort of pervert. I'd say that what's sauce for the goose is sauce for the gander – but, in this context, it might be taken the wrong way.

A woman really shouldn't take any pleasure in the fact that masturbation – invariably with the assistance of hygienic sex aids – is the one area of sexual activity that she's applauded for indulging in while men are derided, because she is indeed being damned with faint praise. Basically, she ain't getting none, and is therefore a Good Girl – albeit one who has several screaming orgasms a night while mauling at her private parts with a piece of plastic, rubber or glass.

The huge growth in the 'sex toy' – again, as with animal-shaped vibrators, yuck; why infantilise an inherently adult desire with this babyish label? – market also indicates that a number of strange women are unwilling to touch themselves 'down there' with the best masturbation tools you'll find on this earth: the two hands the Lord gave you. Somehow, shopping – albeit at Ann Summers – makes it OK, cleanses the sexual impulse, makes you a proper girly girl again.

As someone said – approvingly! – of the eye-wateringly expensive sex shop Myla, 'It's not sex, it's retail therapy.' At the risk of sounding like a bad feminist – oh, you tragic bitches!

THE HYPOCRITICAL GAME

Chas Newkey-Burden

I've loved football since the age of six, but loving football and loving other men has often been an uncomfortable combination. While racism has thankfully been almost eradicated from the game domestically, the stands of stadiums across the country still resound with anti-gay sentiment every weekend. Any player who collapses after a tough challenge is immediately labelled a 'poof' or a 'gay bastard'. Fierce witch-hunts are conducted against players rumoured to be gay, and to accuse an opposing team's player of 'taking it up the arse' is the fan's ultimate insult.

At times the picture gets even gloomier. Tottenham fans sang horrendous songs about Sol Campbell after he made the move across the North London divide. Chants about Campbell, who strongly denies the rumours that have been spread about his sexuality, included several particularly vicious homophobic slurs.

Yet these fans, for whom homosexuality is supposedly the most sickening thing in the world, really need to look at their own behaviour, because they are a bunch of hypocrites. It's they who pay through the nose every other weekend to travel hundreds of miles from their wives and girlfriends and squeeze themselves into cramped stands full of other men.

As we've seen, their obsessive accusation of 'taking it up the arse' is not just directed at players. It sometimes stretches to the players' wives, too. For years, David Beckham infuriated football fans across the country by being better looking and richer than any of them. So what did they do? They took out their fury by chanting 'Posh Spice takes it up the arse' at him at every opportunity. And they say it like it's a bad thing!

It's not just the fans that are hypocrites. As I noted during my years in football journalism, those inside the game are broadly in denial that any player might be gay. It's estimated that at least one in ten people are gay but, despite there currently being over 2,000 professional footballers in Britain, not a single player has come out. The sums just don't work out. But forget the maths; just look at the men! Every week the players shower together and when their team scores a goal they cuddle and kiss and roll around on the grass. Then, if their team has lost, they take their tops off, start crying and hop in the shower together. With recent headlines about 'roasting' scandals, some footballers seem to be taking this a stage further. Is 'roasting' not just two men having sex with each other with a woman in between? Not that I'm jealous, of course.

Before I go and get too gay lib about hypocrisy in football, there's a bit of hypocrisy on the gay side of the fence too. The Gay Football Supporters' Network (GFSN) is a social group for fans who – I always love this – 'happen to be gay'. This oddball bunch are always moaning on about how they are 'real fans' and do not just go to football to look at the players' legs. Then, each year, their members vote for a 'lust league' of sexy players and press release the outcome to all the tabloids. Make your minds up, lads!

There is hypocrisy aplenty among football journalists too, as I discovered during my years in that trade. For so many straight men, following the game is primarily a way of proving to themselves and others that they are not gay. For those who write about it, this is often doubly true. So what did my presence in the ranks say about them? I'll never forget the hypocrisy of one colleague in particular: he was always the first to suggest we wrote articles about campaigns to rid football of racism, and yet I once overheard him saying, 'I've nothing against gay people but there's no place for that sort of person in football.' (I wanted to retort, 'There's no place in football for insecure straight men who haven't had sex for ten years but pick their noses and eat it on a daily basis,' but, of course, you'd only have had to look around our office to prove me wrong!)

The brilliant efforts football has made to rid itself of racism are muddied somewhat by the comparative lack of progress it has made in addressing anti-Semitism. As an Arsenal fan I've become increasingly ashamed by the anti-Semitic chants sung by some of my fellow Gooners. For the uninitiated, Arsenal's local rivals Tottenham Hotspur have had many Jewish fans and directors down the years. This has seen the team labelled as the 'yids' by many football supporters.

True, many Tottenham fans have adopted the 'yids' tag and have chanted 'Yid Army' in support of their team. Many of these would passionately contend that no offence is meant. However, there is no doubt that deep offence is intended by some chants aimed at Tottenham fans by opposing sup-porters. During a match at Manchester United's ground, Spurs fans were greeted by the sound of many United fans hissing at them, in imitation of the sound of gas chambers. Yes, you read that right. In another sickener, an opposing goalkeeper, Mark Bosnich, once performed a Hitler salute in front of the Tottenham fans.

Despite some excellent progress in tackling racism aimed at black players and supporters, anti-Semitism continues to rear its ugly head in football in twenty-first-century Britain. Yet the only real noise made by left-wing groups on Jewish-related football matters has been to slate Arsenal for daring to strike a deal with the Israeli Tourist Board, which promoted Israel as the club's tourist destination of choice. There were predictable calls for boycotts from Palestinian solidarity groups, who are revealingly silent when it is Jewish people who are being discriminated against in football.

Those who shout and scream about Arsenal's deal with Israel, but remain silent about anti-Semitism, might benefit from some reflection too. Arsenal's deal with Israel was applauded loudly in my household. The true shame is the ugly anti-Semitism that is allowed to fester, largely unchallenged, in the supposedly beautiful game.

So, too, is homophobia allowed to run free in a game that kicks its morality out of the window when it comes to anything genuinely worth being offended by. When a player is shamed on the front page rather than praised on the back page of the morning papers, he can normally count on his club and fans forgiving him: our teams have fielded alcoholics, drink-drivers, love rats and wife-beaters. A Premiership player even took to the field wearing an electronic tag, after being released from prison a few days earlier.

So there you have it: the beautiful game laid out in all its hypocritical glory. Beat your wife, wrap your car around a tree, get banged up in jail, but don't, whatever you do, be gay because there's no room for your sort in the game. There's plenty of room for hypocrites, though. In fact, why not buy a season ticket?

And another thing . . .

The hypocrisy that goes hand in hand with football's sexual frustration was played out most vividly during the 2006 World Cup. The wives and girlfriends (WAGS) of the England team were very much part of the story out in Germany. The media loved it and pictures of Cheryl Cole, Victoria Beckham and the majestic Melanie Slade brightened up a dull tournament. Until England were knocked out. Then the same commentators who had spent the previous months discussing the many problems and weaknesses in the England squad suddenly changed their tune: England were the best team in the world and would have won it had it not been for those bleeding WAGS.

THE AGEISM OF THE GAY MAN

Chas Newkey-Burden

Forget bedroom antics; the real pain in the backside about being gay is listening to the incessant whining of older men about how ageist the gay scene is. Visit any gay venue in the country and you'll find a group of men who have pitched up at the bar for an evening of solid drinking and increasingly self-pitying whining about how they are marginalised by a culture that values youth over maturity.

On the face of it, they've got a point: not for nothing is the leading gay listings magazine called *Boyz*. However, they're also a bunch of hypocrites, because the most poisonous ageism of the gay scene is directed not in favour of, but against, the young gay man. And guess who is constantly stirring this pot? Why, it's those poor, marginalised oldies!

I've lost count of the number of old gay men who, when discussing younger gay men, describe them as 'dumb chickens' or 'stupid twinks'. Charming, eh? It's the gay equivalent of the straight man's 'dumb blonde'.

However, were they to race for a gold medal in chauvinism, the gay man would leave his hetero equivalent trailing in his wake. Straight men aren't always angels, of course – many of them consider their sexual prey to be a bit dumb and inferior – but at least they don't simultaneously believe that younger women are involved in some sinister, ageist conspiracy against them. In fact, I don't think I've ever even heard a straight man utter the word 'ageist'. For gay men, however, the same word is as much a part of their vocabulary as 'inches'.

So why, as they get older, are gay men so quick to become the old pots that call the young kettles black? It's a horrible combination of desire and envy. A straight man might ogle a younger woman with a nice pair of tits but that's because he wants to touch those tits, not because he wants a pair of tits like that himself. However, the older gay man both desires and envies the younger gay man's fit body. He wants to 'have' that nice pert bum in both senses of the word.

All too often this leads to a form of attraction that has an uncomfortable level of hatred in it. Wanting both to fuck a younger man and to be a younger man, the ageing gay knows he can only fulfil the first of those dreams, and even then only on a very good day. True, he could always just get over it, but where's the fun in that? Far better to become consumed with bitterness and to accuse the young guys he fancies of the very ageism that he is perpetrating himself. Because, if these poor old souls really are all so upset about ageism, you would think they'd be copping off with each other. But, again, where's the fun in that when you've got a box set of *Euroboyz* and *Twink* DVDs to watch when you get home?

CYCLISTS
Julie Burchill

Way back in 1998, scientists reported that the more a man rode a bicycle, the greater his chance of becoming impotent. You might want to look away now if you're eating, but apparently, when a chap sits on a bike seat, an artery that runs through the perineum, delivering blood to the penis, is squashed. Generally it bounces back – but if it's squished one time too many, it STAYS squished.

Is this the reason cyclists often seem so vile-tempered? (The men, that is; the ladies tend to be more civilised, as per.) All that spitting and swearing and knocking down tots and oldsters alike with their determination to dominate both pavement and road – doesn't it rather smack of a monstrous regiment of Mr Softees seeking to impose their masculinity on the road the way they've failed to in the bed?

Cyclists are hypocrites because they hate drivers, YET THEY ARE DRIVERS! Albeit drivers with extreme prejudice – two wheels good, four wheels bad! And, like a lot of dedicated drivers, they have nothing but contempt for the snail's-pace pedestrian, whom they sometimes accuse of being 'selfish' for 'having space they do not have to share. I don't understand why we can't all share our space,' huffed one cyclist in a letter to the Brighton *Argus*.

Are such people really so cretinous that they cannot grasp how threatening large, fast, wheeled metal objects appear, particularly to the very young and the very old, when they are coming towards a person? Of course, we have Greenery to thank for the rise in the thoroughly selfish sense of empowerment of cyclists – 'I don't cause pollution, therefore I can do as I wish!' the thinking appears to go.

One particular aspect of many of their number's behaviour puzzles us beyond all others, though. Cyclists, as they never tire of letting us know, are in so many ways superior to the rest of us. Indeed, they're so very caring and responsible that the rest of us should be truly ashamed of ourselves for even existing. Just before we flog ourselves to death in sheer molten shame, though, can we please ask, what's with these baby carriers that some cyclist parents stick on the backs of their bikes? Perhaps mere mortals like us 'leggies' have got it wrong, but does a tot really enjoy being positioned where its lungs can take in the maximum amount of traffic fumes from passing cars? How environmentally aware is that?

And, if we may be so bold, oh superior cyclists, can we ask what happens if your mean machine goes under a car while your little darling is strapped into their seat? You'll be lucky enough if you have a few seconds to scramble away and avoid being made into seven cans of cat food. Tot, strapped into the baby carrier, doesn't stand a snowball's. They'll be history – before they could even walk proper! Likewise, if you get hit from behind by a van, you might just live to munch another tofu stir-fry but your toddler has no chance of surviving. Tell me – what's the point in breastfeeding the little bastards till they can open beer cans with their teeth, and then laying them open to such full-on damage?

However, we're sure that, if said tots had actually been old enough to have a say in the matter, they definitely wouldn't have wanted to spend the last moments of their short lives in the safety and comfort of a car. And would obviously instead have wanted their last contribution to this world to be absorbing the impact of a car crash – so their mum or dad could live on to cycle safely another day. Bless!

UGLY SEXIST MEN
Julie Burchill

Some years back, in the late 90s, a brother-and-sister team called John and Catherine Walker invented something called the True Mirror – that is, two 'fine' mirrors fixed together at a strategic angle and sealed in a cube. Apparently these strange-sounding objects quickly became a 'fixture' in 'parts of New York's fashionable East Village', according to *The Times*. Just think, if only that poor mad East Village-dwelling fashion victim played by Sarah Jessica Parker in *Sex and the City* had had such a thing, she might not have continued getting herself up like Baby Jane of *Whatever Happened To?* fame – crossed with a pensive horse – till so late in life.

According to the makers of the True Mirror, most of us prance through life looking like a dog's dinner while thinking we're the cat's pyjamas for the simple reason that most flat, 'backwards' mirrors err in the direction of flattery, especially where the asymmetry of the face is concerned. Though, personally, I don't believe that ordinary mirrors are what stand between us and the true knowledge that these lucid looking glasses might bring; rather, it'll be the Magic Mirror many of us keep at home which will make sure we remain blissfully unaware of reality. Magic Mirrors are mostly owned by men of a certain age, though occasionally a woman with more than her fair share of testosterone will come into possession of this enchanted object – as has been the case with me in the past, tragically. But more of this later.

You may not have ever seen a Magic Mirror, but you'll certainly know a man who has one. The biggest giveaway will be his apparently demented conviction that – even though he invariably has a face like a baboon's bum someone has played a mean game of Mr Potato Head with – not just is an Englishman's home his castle, but this particular man's imagination is his actual harem. He may be a superannuated-lad novelist, an 'alternative' comedian (so alternative that he habitually does reality shows and TV commercials, begging the question 'Alternative to what? NOT being desperate?') or a DJ, but he will have no doubt whatsoever that the entire female population of the world between the ages of sixteen and sixty-one is waiting in an agony of exquisite anticipation to find out whether he finds them 'shaggable' or not.

The old saw about ignorance being bliss finds perhaps its truest, purest expression in this man. His own estimation of his singular sex appeal is so extreme that he will actually spend real, valuable time on 'grading' women, putting them in order of 'do-ability' – Girls Aloud are a favourite sexual smorgas-bord for this picky eater – and even slightly agonise sometimes over which ones he would and wouldn't 'do'. I'll never forget the frankly surreal spectacle a while back of a monumentally unappetising comedian, and a supposedly 'intelligent' one at that, actually differentiating between two beautiful soap opera twins, sex-wise – about how you'd certainly 'give one' to X but, because Y had a 'dodgy eye', this would be on your mind all the while you were 'putting it' to X. Get over it, one felt like crying; it's not gonna happen! Not with the dodgy-eyed twin, not with the pretty-eyed twin, not with anybody's twin except the twin of your own left hand!

I have to say, this is a totally male thing; when I was a size 22, or even now that I'm an ancient 48-year-old size 16, I certainly wouldn't dream of giving interviews in which I carnally ticked the dance cards of notorious male hotties. And it has nothing to do with self-loathing issues, either, or not thinking I am 'good enough' for any old male sex symbol. Indeed, though it grieves me to say it, I cannot tell a lie (except if it's just for cheap kicks, which obviously being a professional to my fingertips it certainly isn't here) and I must admit that when I was huge, I had a bit of a Magic Mirror thing going myself; I couldn't IMAGINE why all those nasty photographers had been so determined to put my sylphlike image through a Fat-Hall-Of-Mirrors distorting machine, or why all the size 12 waistbands had size 22 labels on them.

But be that as it may, my body-dysmorphia-in-reverse ('utorphia'?) was simply a harmless personal foible which allowed me to have a bit of innocent fun teasing 'that fat cow' (as I thought of her; in reality, we'd easily have been able to swop clothes) Dawn French for a bit. Even if I was living in a fool's paradise, it seemed an interesting and rather more mentally healthy twist on the usual delusion of the beauty who thinks she's a beast – you know, Uma Thurman insisting that she looks like a hammerhead shark, or Michelle Pfeiffer practically drawing diagrams to demonstrate that she'd be better employed as Jemima Puddleduck's body-double. This is why Jordan is so hated – Most Hated Living Briton, even, whereas I only came thirtieth or something – with her adorable I'm-hot-get-me! delight in her big toy body; because we are so used to beauty apologising for itself, and forever finding itself wanting. But that way lies poor dead Marilyn – and as a female-friendly feminist, I know which way I'd prefer a girl to go.

Generally, as I've said, men think they are better-looking than they are and women worse – hence my belief in the widespread epidemic of Magic Mirrors. Hollywood has done all it can, of course, to perpetuate this double-standard, which superficially seems to do women down but in the long run makes men look far sillier in their self-delusion – see Jack Nicholson recoiling with horror on encountering an un-dressed Diane Keaton in that film no one remembers the name of, making most sighted members of the audience reflect mirthfully how much more horrid a naked Nicholson would be.

But trust Hollywood's opposite number, Islam, to take things to extremes. I hate to sound like a stand-up comic here (though actually stand-up comics are generally too wussy to take on the Islamofascists) but that Abu Hamza – what does he think he looks like? When he poses for the camera for the nth time with his dodgy eye rolled up in his head and that hook up in front of his face? We may think that he appears to be auditioning for next year's production of *Peter Pan* at the end of Prestatyn pier, but I bet you any money that he's thinking, 'Gosh, but I look well cool and hard – move over, Omar Sharif! That Jodie Marsh, eh? Ruff, ruff! Wouldn't touch her with yours, mate!'

Now that's a Magic Mirror and a half.

FOREIGN AFFAIRS

Iraq: Not In My Name; Drooling Fetishisation of Arab Brutality, Sexism and Racism/Ceaseless Whining about Alleged Israeli Brutality, Sexism And Racism; Israel Haters; Cuba; George Bush Bashers; Anti-Americanism; Catholic Hypocrisy

IRAQ: NOT IN MY NAME

Chas Newkey-Burden

In February 2003, one of the most hypocritical gatherings in mankind's history took place in London. Millions took advantage of Britain's freedom and democracy, marching through the streets to ask that the government deprive Iraqi people of those very values. Lest anyone mistake the marchers' fury as being primarily motivated by any admirable qualities, they marched under the most narcissistic, self-centred and revealing of slogans: Not In My Name.

Amid all the accounts of hypocritical deception that are plastered over the pages of this book, I suppose we should be fair and take a moment to tip our hats to the sheer honesty of this sound bite. It might have been breathtakingly selfish but it made absolutely no bones about it. However, the honesty of the slogan aside, there was oodles of hypocrisy in the antiwar movement.

The 2003 march brought allsorts to the capital: from seasoned leftie protestors to *Daily Mail* readers and everyone in between. It was the same 'we just felt we had to be here' mentality that occurred when Princess Diana died, though this time far less admirably motivated. Indicative of this mentality was the fact that alongside the Not In My Name placards was another which read 'No War — Freedom For Palestine'. It's safe to say that many of the marchers would have struggled to say what 'Palestine' is or was, let alone be able even to begin to outline what freedom for Palestine would entail for the region.

Particularly well represented among those who just felt they had to be there were the chattering classes, and in joining the antiwar bandwagon, they managed to contradict many of their own supposedly deeply held values. As they had sat around their dinner tables during the previous six years, many of these people had railed against Tony Blair for his obsession with spin. They accused him of having no backbone or principles. They sniggered at his use of focus groups. When, they wondered, would he stop seeking approval for everything he did?

However, come the build-up to Iraq, and one of the central planks of these people's opposition to the war was their fury that Blair wasn't seeking enough approval. Suddenly, he was too stubborn and wasn't listening to his people enough. In an amusing moment of getting totally the wrong end of the stick, a *Guardian* columnist described the war as 'a crushing blow to democracy'. Indignant demonstrators felt the same and asked, 'Haven't you heard of democracy, Mr Blair?'

Yes he had, and he wanted to make sure Iraqi children got to hear of it too. With Iraq, Blair threw out of the window his obsessions with spin, approval and short-term gain. In doing so, Britain's youngest-ever prime minister truly came of age as a leader and a man. In contrast to when Thatcher went to war for the people of the Falkland Islands, Blair knew full well that his stance on Iraq was never going to reap electoral dividends. He also knew it could wreck his legacy. In making his stance, he demonstrated all manner of qualities that he'd previously only shown in spasms: he was steadfast, courageous and self-sacrificing. None of these qualities is one that the modern hypocrite possesses to any significant degree at all; no wonder they were so puzzled by Blair's action.

As we've seen, their hypocrisy was without shame. They demanded more democracy at home in order to prevent the Iraqis getting any democracy at all. They took advantage of their right to march in protest against government policy in order to prevent Iraqis from ever being able to express any protest whatsoever against their dictator's policies. Because, make no mistake about it, that was the natural conclusion of their wishes.

Their obsession with the importance of democracy and freedom at home starkly contradicts their passion for depriving Iraqis of those same values. What's good enough for us isn't good enough for the Iraqis. We were told that you cannot force democracy and freedom on people, especially on Arab countries. Taking this hideous, racist argument to its natural conclusion, it could be argued that not since the far right marched through the streets of East London had the capital seen such a public demonstration of whites-first sentiment. However, at least the far right had the honesty and self-awareness to admit to themselves and others where their racist priorities lay. Hell will freeze over before any of the antiwar bunch are as honest about their own wicked manifesto. How ironic too that the antiwar drum was beaten so loudly by 'groovy' comedians. How long did these clowns think they would survive as comedians and film-makers in Saddam's Iraq before the dictator tortured them to death?

Many of those who marched against war in Iraq are the same people who also protest against planned infringements of civil liberties in England. They screamed blue murder at suggestions of ID cards, policies that increased the amount of time terror suspects could be held without charge, and changes in the rules governing surveillance. How revealing that the only things to get these people off their backsides and onto the streets are to oppose any suggestion of a decrease in civil liberties at home or to oppose any suggestion of an increase of civil liberties for Iraqi people.

Indeed, one of the anti-ID card brigade showed his true colours when he arrived in an office I was working in on the morning of 7 July 2005. On being informed that terrorists were slaughtering people across the London Transport system, he rolled his eyes and said, 'Oh no, this is going to be terrible for the ID-card campaign.' Elsewhere that day, people stomped around saying, 'This is all Tony Blair's fault,' as if the terrorists who blow themselves and others up are lovely people who just can't help but be controlled by Blair's policies. When there are no terror attacks, the left attack the government for creating 'scare stories' about non-existent terror threats and getting the whole thing out of proportion. Then, when people are slaughtered across London, suddenly the government have not been taking the terror threat seriously enough.

Iraq was a colossally huge and important issue and, clearly, the natural consequences of both sides of the argument came with a horrendous price to pay: the pro-war side had to accept that there would be loss of civilian life if they had their way; while the antiwar side had to accept that Saddam Hussein, leader of the Ba'ath Party, whose Syrian founders were heavily influenced by Nazism, would remain in power if they had theirs. Here's the thing, though: I've never met a single pro-war person who failed to accept the consequences of their argument. Similarly, I've never met a single antiwar person who *did* accept the consequences of theirs.

On a broader level, the consequences of the antiwar movement's demands would also mean that the Taliban would still be in charge in Afghanistan, flogging to death any woman caught without a burka and executing any woman who tried to get an education after the age of eight. Saddam Hussein would still be terrorising and torturing the people of Iraq and would be several steps closer to acquiring those weapons he was negotiating with North Korea for immediately prior to his downfall. Nobody could suggest that the war has been an unqualified success, but let's be clear about this: the antiwar movement were opposed to the war whether it proved to be a success or not.

You'd think that even the bitterest opponent of the war would be able to accept that the removal of Saddam Hussein was in itself a wonderful moment in the history of mankind. Sadly, this was not the case, and the hypocrisy that greeted the execution of Saddam absolutely stank. For years, the antiwar bunch had been insisting that the many executions in the Middle East were not something that we should criticise. 'It's just their culture,' we were told condescendingly, as gay men were hung in public squares, and women were stoned to death to punish them for being raped. However, when a mass-murdering dictator was put to death for his crimes, suddenly the death sentence was barbaric. (It's also safe to say that, if a British prime minister made a concerted effort to bring the death sentence in over here, those who refuse to condemn its use in Arab states would suddenly find all manner of reasons to oppose it at home.)

But then these types were always magnificent at rhetorical gymnastics. When we first went after Osama Bin Laden in Afghanistan, they blabbered on about 'innocent until proven guilty' and questioned whether we had the right to be chasing Bin Laden at all. However, once we went into Iraq, suddenly many of these people became convinced that Bin Laden had been a correct target to chase after all. Now, the only thing wrong with our targeting of Bin Laden was that we were not putting enough resources into it, and the Iraq war was billed as a distraction from the hunt for Bin Laden, who was the real enemy. Similarly, those who opposed sending any troops to Afghanistan and Iraq have since complained that we did not send enough. There is literally no consistency to these people's beliefs other than a hatred towards, and envy of, America.

Because in truth, anti-Americanism seems to be the only consideration they give the matter. I've rarely met an antiwar person who seemed to have wrestled over or considered at any length at all their stance. Indeed, there seemed to be almost a jubilation to their opposition, as Ian McEwan outlined so well in his novel *Saturday*. Likewise, in his fantastic diaries, Alastair Campbell recounts how he went for a run on the afternoon of the demonstration and 'bumped into no end of people coming back from the march, placards under arms, faces full of self-righteousness'.

As these people jubilantly returned from their march across the streets of London, Saddam Hussein made it known that he was overjoyed to hear of their demonstration. So thrilled was he that he arranged for Iraqi television to show footage of the marches to his terrified public. I try and meet people halfway, but how on earth can anybody have been proud to have been on a march that was cheered all the way by Saddam Hussein?

But then perhaps it makes sense that many who opposed the Iraq war also find it so easy to shrug off Iran's President Ahmadinejad's plans to slaughter millions of Jews. After all, many opponents of Iraq were quick to position the Iraq war as 'the Jewish war'. Thereby did these activists – many of whom would claim to be virulent anti-racists – once more show their true hypocritical colours.

If I seem to be proposing harsh motives on the antiwar movement, it's only because, try as I might, I struggle to see their agenda in any other terms. For instance, I can fully understand why someone who feels that Muslims don't deserve or cannot cope with democracy would instinctively oppose the Iraq war. But I cannot see how anyone who believes that freedom and democracy are universal human values, deserved by everyone, would be so quick and fundamental in their opposition to the war.

Likewise, I can understand why someone who is anti-Semitic would try and portray the war as some sort of sinister Jewish conspiracy. I struggle to find any more reasonable, fair-minded motives for this sort of poisonous lie. (Incidentally, while it's safe to say that few in Israel mourned the end of a dictator who funded the suicide bombers that blew their people up, plenty in Israel opposed the Iraq war, largely on the grounds that Iran was the more pressing threat.)

So what would the antiwar movement have done about the threat of apocalyptic terror and brutal dictatorial regimes that torture and murder their own people? Meanwhile, CND veteran campaigner Bruce Kent said in the aftermath of the 9/11 attacks, 'I think we need to pursue Bin Laden in different ways . . . I would even go as far as combing through bank accounts across the world and freezing anything suspicious.'

Ooh, Bruce, you mean you'd actually open a letter that wasn't addressed to you? That'll show al-Qaeda!

In closing, let's return to that slogan which gave this book its title. 'Not in my name,' they chanted, revealing everything about their motives. Their opposition had little concern for the Iraqi people but bucket loads of concern for themselves. As my co-author wrote at the time, 'Who gives a stuff about their wet, white, Western names?' Absolutely, and the more you examine it, the more hypocrisy is revealed. In May 1997, many of these people danced the night away as Tony Blair brought to an end two decades of Conservative rule. Now at last, they cheered, the 'me, me, me' of Thatcherism would be replaced by something better. Yet surely even Thatcher herself would have balked at the 'me, me, me' of Not In My Name. Earlier in this essay, I praised the slogan for its honesty but, on reflection, I'd like to qualify my praise, because surely a truly honest slogan for this march would be 'Keep Saddam In Power'.

A far more dignified sentiment was offered by Iraqi exile Shanaz Rashid at the Labour Party conference in 2004 as opposition to the war grew. Rashid told how she had, in the aftermath of Iraq's liberation, landed at Baghdad airport, kissed the ground and wept for her freedom, 'freedom that you take for granted!' She also told the conference that, 'You may feel you can attack your leader, but it is Mr Blair who has stood up to Saddam and has freed my people!' Saddam had, after all, tortured and murdered her relatives.

As Simon Hoggart reported in the *Guardian*:

> By this time her face, viewed on the two giant screens, had crumpled with a mixture of rage, frustration and relief.

'Yes, there have been difficulties, yes, there have been mistakes, perhaps many mistakes. No, you didn't find weapons of mass destruction. But, for the great majority of Iraqis, WMD were never an issue. We never understood the argument about them.

'All we wanted was to be free! Free! FREE!' she cried, her voice peaking dangerously as TV sound engineers ripped off their earphones and stuffed tissues up their bleeding noses. 'Please, please, do not desert us in our hour of need!'

Nobody knew how to cope. As Ms Rashid fled from the stage, all passion spent, she was followed by a Marian Grimes from Edinburgh, whose voice was as low and mumbly as Ms Rashid's was high-pitched and furious.

'I'm finding it very difficult to follow that,' she said, but she soon found a way: she simply ignored it, and didn't address a single point that Ms Rashid had made. Nor did any of the troops-out-now people. They simply pretended she hadn't been there.

And another thing . . .

If the Iraq issue brought out the worst in some people, then the same is true of the question of Iran's nuclear ambitions. Whatever ultimately happens with the Iran nuclear issue, the abiding memory of the debate will always be the instances of otherwise intelligent, humanitarian people going into the most sickening state of denial when it comes to Ahmadinejad's frequent threats to nuke Israel. 'But Iran's been saying that for years,' they shrug, 'I don't think they're serious'. Yes, Iran's been saying it for years. But it is now preparing the means to see it through. In the last century, the world sat back as millions of Jews were killed by a dictator, and now people are sitting back again, content to 'see how it pans out'. Look at how little we've learned.

Writing on the excellent First Post website, Matthew Carr exemplified this blinkered vision. Pouring scorn on the rumoured preparations for an attack on Iran's nuclear facilities, he wrote, 'Expect dehumanising rhetoric about nuclear-armed "mad Mullahs", attacks on US troops by "Iranian-backed" insurgents, talk of "Islamo-fascism" and women's rights, of clashing civilisations and the need to act sooner not later. There will, too, be endless replays of Ahmadinejad's mistranslated quote about "wiping Israel off the map".'

Carr's biography on the website reveals that he lives in Derbyshire. One wonders whether he would be able to maintain his denial about Ahmadinejad's nuclear sabre-rattling against Israel if he lived not in Derbyshire but in, say, the centre of Tel Aviv? Also, if Carr were female, would he be quite so swift to comment on 'talk of . . . women's rights' and Islamo-fascism?

DROOLING FETISHISATION OF ARAB BRUTALITY, SEXISM AND RACISM/ CEASELESS WHINING ABOUT ALLEGED ISRAELI BRUTALITY, SEXISM AND RACISM

Julie Burchill

Exactly where do you go after Kylie or Gisele – after having more than one man should have, sexually, in his lifetime before you even hit forty? In the case of Olivier Martinez and Leonardo DiCaprio, they went Israeli, in the shape of Sarai Givati and Bar Rafael respectively.

But the lure of these unique people goes a lot further than the undoubted appeal of a brace of tasty pin-up girls. Admiring Israel in any way possible seems to me to be a natural, healthy reaction to, and rebellion against, the ceaseless Muslim-sucking, Arab-licking propaganda spewed out by the rest of the British arts and media, which often seems to reach unwholesomely parasexual heights of frenzy.

Western fetishising of Arab brutality has always been an embarrassment to those of us who prefer to be led by our brains rather than genitalia. It started with the ludicrous TE Lawrence, going native for love of the lash and invariably following his cock into regional conflicts – as he said, 'I liked a particular Arab [a fourteen-year-old boy, apparently; charming!] and thought that freedom for the race would be an acceptable present.' Mr Ambassador, with your high-handed fast-and-loose shifting of national borders, you are spoiling us!

Showbiz was as prey to all this silliness as politics in this matter, and in 1922 Rudolph Valentino as The Sheikh whisked some wide-eyed masochist off for a good old ravish in his desert abode as imagined in the eponymous book by Elinor Glyn. The previous year had seen a hit song, 'The Sheikh of Araby', in which our desert chums were already showing signs of the 'that's-mine-I'm-having-it' tendency which blights the Middle East to this very day, with lines like 'Your love belongs to me', 'At night when you're asleep, into your tent I'll creep' and 'You'll rule this land with me' – steady on!

Here's the crux of the problem. Of course it's not the fault of any given ethnic or cultural group if weird white folk who aren't getting off at home choose to perv over them. But – and it's a big belly-dancing but! – in this case at least, there has been just a teeny-weeny bit of fact to base the fantasy on. Arabs had harems, though now they call it polygamy. They ride camels, given half a chance – or, rather, set bartered boy children to ride them, thus pulling in even more of the infidel's holiday money.

But are Arabs as sexy as some weird Brits insist on finding them? You wouldn't think so, reading about how they'll stone some poor broad to death for the deadly sin of showing her chin – oh, shameless hussy! On the contrary, modern Arab Muslims are outrageous Mrs Grundys, always ready to see shame where only flesh exists. Any day now, some previously 'liberal, reforming' king of a Gulf state will surely ban photos of blue tits, the bird kind, on the basis that they're causing seven sorts of rumpus beneath the dish-doshes of the nation's blameless males.

So sexually inhibited are the Muslim Arab nations, in fact, that in 2005 the Home Office refused to let a young British woman use a particular photograph of her seven-month-old son in his first passport as it might have been considered 'offensive' to Muslim countries. Why? BECAUSE THE LITTLE HE-HUSSY WAS TOPLESS!

On paper, many of these drooling fetishists are pro-democratic, pro-underdog, pro-progress. So what on earth could explain their ceaseless, irrational, supremely hypocritical habit of favouring the filthily rich gang of Arab dictatorships over the ever-struggling, always democratic state of Israel?

I blame the subliminal power of advertising myself. All through the 70s and 80s and right into the 90s, one of the most popular of all British TV commercials was that one for Fry's Turkish Delight, during which, in various permutations, a doe-eyed bint – sexy chiffon veil masking her lower face, but naturally none of the grim reality of the burka, which leaves a lady looking like a parrot cage that someone forgot to uncover; soooo not a good look – welcomed a suave, dish-dosh-wearing gent into her tent, there to share said gooey pink substance with him.

Who's to say that the British Islamo-groupies weren't swept off their feet by this flamboyant display of Mohammedan concupiscence? Of course, even before the Turkish Delight chick commenced to fill her boots on prime-time TV, a certain sort of seat-sniffing Westerner was tripping on the idea of the noble-savage-sheikh who would free them of all their Judaeo-Christian hang-ups. Of course, all sexual fantasies say more about what the fantasist lacks than what the object of fantasy actually has – but, at a time when even seven-month-old babies are forced to cover their tiny nipples in order not to offend the all-evil-seeing eye of Islam, how singularly inaccurate this one in particular seems!

We'd surely make more sense fetishising ugly Swedes or teetotal Celts than sexy Arabs. And meanwhile, relaxed, pluralist, sexy Israel goes quietly about its business. Whether being represented by a transsexual singer at Eurovision, giving Miss Israel special dispensation not to carry her assault rifle during national service because she says it bruises her legs or holding International Pride right there in Jerusalem, their attitude to matters sexual is a breath of fresh air in a deeply rancid region. And this isn't even taking into consideration the amazing beauty of its people; not for nothing does my enchanting collaborator Mr N-B refer to his first trip there – just short of a week – as The Six Day Phwoar.

Despite the vicious lies about Israel being the natural heir to apartheid-era South Africa, no country ever boasted such a rainbow of beauty, from the black-skinned Falashas to the blonds of Scandinavian extraction. What a contrast to the slave-owning, racism-condoning Islamic countries surrounding it! And what a welcome antidote to the decades of sexual stereotypes imposed on the Jews by jealous Gentiles – the ugly nerd who has to rely on his wits and his cash to get laid, and the ball-breaking Jewish yenta nagging her menfolk into impotence. Israel dismantles all the dirty prejudices fostered over the centuries of diaspora, and reveals them as born-again beauties, standing proud in the sunlight of self-determination.

At the end of the day, it's hard to control what turns you on and so long as it doesn't say 'quack' or 'I'm five', it's a free world. But I can't help thinking it's a bit sad – not to mention hypocritical, considering all the abuse Israel gets for being horrid and nasty in every way a country can be horrid and nasty – that Arab fetishisers prize cruelty in their fantasy men and submission in their fantasy women. That is boring old sexism with bells on.

Whereas we Israeli-lovers, on the other hand, celebrate flexibility, modernity and true diversity. And a damn good uniform.

ISRAEL HATERS
Chas Newkey-Burden

'When my father was a little boy in Poland, the streets of Europe were covered with graffiti, "Jews, go back to Palestine," or sometimes worse: "Dirty Yids, piss off to Palestine." When my father revisited Europe fifty years later, the walls were covered with new graffiti, "Jews, get out of Palestine."'

Israeli author Amos Oz

Everyone knows the proverb of the three wise monkeys who see no evil, hear no evil and speak no evil. As shown throughout this book, the modern hypocrite can be very skilled indeed at seeing and hearing no evil. When women are stoned to death in Arab states, when gay men are brutalised in Caribbean countries, the hypocrites' ability to cover their ears and look the other way is remarkable.

However, the triumvirate cannot be completed, for when it comes to the state of Israel the modern hypocrite just cannot stop speaking evil. They will fail to condemn – and sometimes actually support – terrorists who blow up school buses and pizza parlours. They will march hand in hand with people who – quite literally – fundamentally disagree with every basic political principle they claim to hold dear. They will openly question whether Israel even has the right to exist.

And all along the way, they will show themselves to be devastating hypocrites. The anti-Israel brigade would have us believe that the motivation for this vitriolic hatred of Israel is a genuine, compassionate concern for the fate of the Palestinian people. But do they really care about the Palestinians, or is their compassion somewhat selective, to put it politely? In reality, are they only interested in Palestinian suffering for as long as it gives them an opportunity to bash Israel?

This hypocrisy is not entirely modern. When the West Bank and the Gaza Strip were occupied by Jordan and Egypt, those occupations of Palestinian land drew not a whimper of protest from the people who spat blood at the 'occupation' of those territories by Israel. When Jordan killed thousands of Palestinians and drove just as many of them from their refugee camps into Lebanon, Israel-bashers saw nothing wrong with that at all. Neither did they take issue with Kuwait when it deported Palestinians in the aftermath of the 1991 Iraq war. Why were they silent in all these cases? Because none of them gave them a chance to bash Israel, of course.

Well established as this hypocrisy is, in the twenty-first century it has well and truly taken root, as 'supporting' the Palestinians has become achingly fashionable. So when Hamas-sparked violence led to Palestinian students at a West Bank university being brutally beaten and shot by their own people, the Westerners who claim to support the Palestinians raised not a single word of protest or concern. Similarly, when Palestinian women are stabbed to death in 'honour killings' across the West Bank and Gaza Strip, no anti-Israel Westerners lose a single moment's sleep on their behalf.

Likewise, when Palestinian children are hospitalised after being caught in the crossfire of fighting between rival Palestinian factions, there is not a word of condemnation from the West. When Palestinian children are deliberately forced into the line of fire by their own people, where is the concern from those in the West who claim to be their biggest supporters? When terrorists are found to be hiding hand grenades in the cradles where Palestinian babies sleep, where is the outrage?

If Israelis are accused of torturing Palestinian terror suspects, the hypocrite is indignantly up in arms in protest without establishing a single fact, but when Palestinians suspected of collaborating are proven to be brutally tortured – sometimes to death – by members of Islamic Jihad, again the silence is deafening.

Similarly, if these people are truly concerned about the Palestinians, then where are their words of praise for Israel when it flings open its hospital doors to them? Just one example: in May 2007 an eight-day-old baby from the Gaza

Strip that was suffering with congenital heart complications was treated in a hospital in Israel. An Israeli Magen David Adom (their equivalent of the Red Cross) ambulance drove into the Gaza Strip, dodging Qassam rockets that were heading for Israel and collected the child for treatment at the Sheba Medical Centre in Tel-Hashomer, near Tel Aviv. Such cases are far from rare. But I've never heard a word of praise for these treatments from any of those in the West who claim to be concerned over the fate of the Palestinians.

It's the same with the refugee question. The heartbreak that the hypocrite feels for Palestinian refugees is only expressed in the context of slamming Israel. When it's pointed out to them that the Arab world has done precious little to help the refugees, their interest dwindles. And what of the hundreds and thousands of Jewish refugees who were deported from Arab states? They've never received any compensation – as Palestinian refugees have from Israel – and no Westerner has lost sleep on their behalf.

Any action taken by Israel to deal with Palestinian terrorists is met with abuse and distortion. The case of Jenin was typical. Following scores of suicide bombings organised from within the Jenin refugee camp, Israel entered the camp in 2002 in search of the terrorists. As the fighting ended the media leaped into action to demonise Israel's action. The *Guardian* described Israel's actions as 'every bit as repellent' as the 9/11 attacks. The *Evening Standard* cried, 'We are talking here of massacre, and a cover-up, of genocide.' The *Independent* spoke of a 'war crime' and *The Times* claimed there were 'mass graves'. The head of the United Nations Refugee Agency was quickly out of the traps to describe the affair as a 'human rights catastrophe that has few parallels in recent history'. The EU was not far behind in its condemnation.

Let's examine the facts of this massacre, this genocide. In total 75 people died at Jenin: 23 of these were Israeli soldiers, and 52 were Palestinians, almost all of them combatants. By even the most hysterical, loaded standards of language this does not constitute genocide, nor anything of the sort. Indeed, the Palestinian death toll would have been much higher – and the Israeli death toll non-existent – had Israel simply bombed the camp from the air. Instead, to avoid civilian casualties, Israel put their own soldiers at risk, sending them in on foot to search through booby-trapped homes.

When Prime Minister Ariel Sharon next visited Israeli troops, one of them asked him, 'Why didn't we bomb the terrorists from the air? That operation cost the lives of more than twenty of our comrades!' Sharon replied, 'That is the painful and inevitable price that those who refuse to abandon their humanity have to pay.' In return for paying the painful price of eschewing air attacks, Sharon and the brave Israeli soldiers who entered a terrorist camp on foot were accused of genocide and massacre and spoken of in the same terms as the 9/11 terrorists.

However, the hypocrisy doesn't end there. In 2007, another Palestinian camp, which had become swamped with suicide bombers, was attacked. This time, the gloves came off. The camp was surrounded by tanks and artillery that fired indiscriminately at the inhabitants. Snipers backed up this fire. The camp's water and electricity supplies were cut off. Thousands of innocent Palestinians were forced to flee but not before at least eighteen had been killed and dozens injured. The camp itself was reduced to rubble. Ultimately, the fighting killed more than 300 people and forced nearly 40,000 Palestinian refugees to flee.

This time, there was next to no coverage in the British media. There was no talk of genocide or massacre. Rather than condemning the attack, the EU and UN were quick to express their support to the army. Even the Arab League came out in support. So what had changed? You guessed it, this time the army dealing with the camp was not the Israeli army but the Lebanese army. How terrifyingly revealing this is of the hypocrisy of those who claim to care about the fate of the Palestinians.

During the fighting, tanks and artillery had also fired at residential areas of Lebanon and civilians were inevitably caught in the crossfire. Just months earlier, the antiwar brigade had been marching through the streets of London to express their concern for the people of Lebanon who were caught in the crossfire of Israel's fighting with Hezbollah. Strangely, the marchers couldn't get off their self-righteous backsides when Lebanese civilians were being shot at by Islamic groups: this time, the people of Lebanon could go to hell as far as they were concerned.

How different it had been in the summer of 2006. 'We are all Hezbollah now,' the modern hypocrites had chanted as they marched in fury against Israel's latest battle for survival, as the rockets of that terror group were raining down on its cities and kibbutzim. If 'Not In My Name' was an embarrassing slogan, then 'We are all Hezbollah now' was little short of insane. How could these marchers, who say they oppose misogyny, tyranny, homophobia and genocide, march in support of an organisation that fanatically and brutally promotes all those things? Because they're hypocrites, of course, and because their frenzied hatred of Israel has utterly stupefied them. It was embarrassing for them, therefore, when Hezbollah's leader Hassan Nasrallah told them, 'We don't want anything from you. We just want to eliminate you.' As Martin Amis neatly put it, these demonstrators were 'up the arse of the people that want them dead'.

But what were they doing up there? Many no doubt believed that during the war they were backing the little guy of Hezbollah against the big guy of Israel. The truth was somewhat different, though. Hezbollah was no little guy; it was backed by millions of pounds of Iranian and Syrian money. Neither were the two sides of the conflict as clear-cut as they believed. The Israeli Arabs of Haifa spent much of the summer sitting in bunkers to avoid being killed by Hezbollah rockets. Many of these Arabs cheered on the Israeli army throughout the campaign. Similarly, Ethiopian Jews whom Israel had previously bravely airlifted from oppression and starvation were particularly badly hit in Tiberias. How incredible that, back in England, many of the groups whose members wear white 'Make Poverty History' wristbands and campaign on Third World debt were willing to cheer as Ethiopians were bombed by Hezbollah.

So no, Israel was not necessarily the Goliath of the conflict. How could a nation the size of Wales, surrounded by millions who want it wiped off the map, be a Goliath? However, the courage shown by its soldiers was immense. Lt Col Roe Klein was marching at the head of a unit of troops when a Hezbollah man threw a hand grenade at them. Lt Klein jumped on top of the grenade to save his troops, losing his life in the process. Meanwhile, Hezbollah were employing the standard cowardly tactic of hiding among women and children, with wheelchair-bound people a particular favourite.

Throughout Israel, the population showed itself to be as brave and humanitarian as ever. Newspapers were full of classified advertisements in which families offered to house those from the north of the country who were under Hezbollah fire. Ultra-Orthodox Jews took in secular Jews; people living in small flats flung open their doors to large families with pets. The Blitz spirit also saw youngsters from the big cities like Jerusalem and Tel Aviv organise treats for Arab children from Galilee. The government arranged for celebrities to visit the bunker-ridden population of the north and even flew in a gay porn star to cheer up gay Israeli troops. As Hezbollah's rockets rained down over northern Israel, weddings in the region had to be cancelled. So cinema producer Eliman Bardugo arranged for those affected to have the chance to be married en masse on the beach in Tel Aviv. Some fifty couples took him up on the offer.

Meanwhile, in London, left-wing people took to the streets to cheer on Hezbollah as it butchered Israeli people. As, for instance, a Hezbollah rocket hit a kibbutz and killed twelve people including an ultra-Orthodox Jew who was sitting next to a hippy with pierced ears. The more these incidents happened, the further the marchers climbed up the arses of the people who wanted them dead. It would have been familiar territory for many of them.

When I went to see the play *My Name Is Rachel Corrie* in London's West End, I sat in an audience littered with white English men and women wearing keffiyeh scarves, some wearing Hamas badges. I see these people – and the marching Hezbollah-wannabes – as terror groupies, a sort of left-wing equivalent of the little boys who play army in playgrounds across England. But these are adults, so they really should know better.

I'm not sure the terror groupies look the other way on the topic of Palestinian terrorism. They seem – sorry to say – almost turned on by it. You surely can't, after all, overlook something as big as the blowing up of buses or pizza parlours. There is no 'bigger picture' regarding people who do that. And why would you appropriate the uniform of the man who backed all that terrorism unless you actively had, well, a bit of a thing for him? For much of the audience, the play about Rachel Corrie must have been a gleefully pornographic experience. They say a picture is worth a thousand words but sometimes a picture can be worth far more than that. There are more than a thousand words in the play, about Corrie, the young US activist who accidentally died during an anti-Israel protest in Gaza in 2003. But none of them shed light on the now-canonised Corrie as much as a photograph taken of her by the Associated Press a month before her death. She was snapped burning an American flag and whipping up the crowd at a pro-Hamas rally.

Naturally, there is no mention of this photograph in the play. Neither is it mentioned that, thanks in part to demonstrations of the International Solidarity Movement with whom Corrie travelled to the Middle East, the Israel Defence Force was prevented from blocking the passage of weapons that were later shown to have been used to kill Israeli children in southern Israel.

Instead, the play is full of naive anti-Israel propaganda from the mouth of Corrie. 'The vast majority of Palestinians right now, as far as I can tell, are engaging in Gandhian non-violent resistance,' she wrote in 2003 as Palestinian suicide bombs were slaughtering Israelis. Lest we forget who the real star of the story is, towards the end of the play Corrie writes, 'When I come back from Palestine I probably will have nightmares and constantly feel guilty for not being here, but I can channel that into more work.' We're back in self-indulgence territory, aren't we? Not in my name. My name is Rachel Corrie. We're all Hezbollah now. Thousands are dying but it's all about me. The hypocrisy of the audience was depressing. I wonder if any were even aware that Hamas had danced over Corrie's grave when she died? To the Palestinians, a dead young American girl was a wonderful publicity coup. Had any of the audience travelled to the Middle East in a Corrie-esque trip of self-indulgence, the Palestinians would have crossed their fingers in the hope they too died.

As I say, the modern hypocrite is delighted to overlook misogyny, homophobia and brutal clampdowns on all manner of personal freedoms in Arab states, and the other side of this coin of hypocritical currency is the way they simultaneously overlook the extraordinarily positive record Israel has on such issues. Take the case of Golda Meir, Israel's first female prime minister who took the top job in 1969, just twenty-one years into the country's existence and a full decade before we in the UK had our first female leader. In some Arab states, women are not allowed to go to school. In Israel they can become the most powerful person in the country.

Meir herself was well aware of this spectacular contrast. In 1948, when she was a negotiator with the Jewish Agency, she set off on a mission to meet King Abdullah of Transjordan. The meeting was secret so she travelled with the Agency's Arab expert Ezra Danin and posed as his wife. She recalled, 'I would travel in the traditional dark and voluminous robes of an Arab woman. I spoke no Arabic at all but as a Moslem wife accompanying her husband it was most unlikely that I would be called upon to say anything to anyone.' How hypocritical it is of those left-wingers in the West that they can hate a country with tales such as these throughout its history.

It's just the same with gay issues. Left-wingers who say they passionately believe in gay rights manage to put that passion aside when it comes to their view of the only country in the Middle East with a positive record on the issue. A wonderfully positive record, in fact. In 2006, within days of the country's fighting with Hezbollah ending, I flew to Israel to research a feature on gay life in the Holy Land. Before leaving, I'd been warned by anti-Israel Westerners to expect to find a very homophobic country. Had any of them bothered to visit Israel, they'd have discovered it's nothing of the sort. Workplace discrimination against gay people is outlawed; the Knesset (Israel's parliament) has openly gay members; in schools, teenagers learn about the difficulties of being gay and the importance of treating all sexualities equally. The Israel Defence Force has dozens of openly gay officers who, like all gay soldiers in its ranks, are treated equally by order of the government.

The Supreme Court has ruled that gay couples are eligible for spousal and widower benefits. The country has gay football teams. Most mainstream television dramas in Israel regularly feature gay storylines. When transsexual Dana International won the 1998 Eurovision Song Contest as Israel's representative, 80 per cent of polled Israelis called her 'an appropriate representative of Israel'.

These facts are there for all to see but it is only on visiting Israel that you discover how happily the different sections of society coexist. I interviewed a gay Israeli man on Tel Aviv's 'Hilton beach' – it is opposite the Hilton hotel – which is also known as the 'gay beach', where men openly check each other out and pick each other up. It is neighboured by the city's religious beach, which has separate bathing days for men and women. And all this is just yards from Tel Aviv's Independence Park, which is the main gay cruising area in Tel Aviv. The cruising park in Jerusalem has the same name.

Elsewhere in Tel Aviv is the House of Freedom. Opened in the late 1990s, this is a shelter for gay, lesbian and transgender youngsters between the ages of twelve and eighteen who have been thrown out of their homes after coming out to their parents. At the House they are counselled by social workers, who then visit the parents and attempt to bring about reconciliation. Those attempts are often successful, and each year hundreds of gay youngsters return to a better home thanks to this remarkable institution.

And everywhere you go in the city, gay men walk hand in hand more openly than they would even in London's Soho. It is staggering that Western left-wingers who claim to believe in gay rights can be so furiously opposed to tolerant Israel. The tolerance is not confined to Tel Aviv, either. When some in Jerusalem opposed the staging of the gay pride parade in the capital in 2007, the Western media presented a city on the brink of civil war. I happened to be in Jerusalem that week – though I didn't attend the parade – and I saw no unrest. Perhaps the strongest opposition I witnessed to the parade came from a taxi driver. I asked him what he thought about it and he sighed deeply before saying, 'Oh, it was terrible for the traffic.' He was right, too!

By hating Israel, the pro-gay-rights left are not just proving to be hypocritical, they are also endangering the one hope that gay Palestinians have. The leading gay rights organisation in Israel organises Arabic gay evenings where gay Palestinians from the West Bank and Gaza Strip are invited to come and party with Israelis – and many take up the invitation. 'We are their only hope,' says one of the organisers. 'If they came out where they live, they would be killed, but they can come and party with us in Israel.' As has been documented by human rights groups, gay Palestinians are routinely tortured and murdered by their own people. They often flee to the safety of Israel.

The attraction that Israel should hold for believers in the rainbow alliance doesn't end with its record on women and gay men. I remember, on a road trip from the Dead Sea to Tel Aviv, marvelling at a quartet of an ultra-Orthodox Jew, an Arab, a uniformed Israeli soldier and a miniskirt-wearing girl in her late teens all engaging in friendly chit-chat as they waited for some traffic lights to change. Such sights are far from uncommon as Israel is home to one of the planet's most diverse people: dreadlocked Ethiopians, and their fellow Africans from Yemen, Egypt and Morocco exist alongside people from Iraq, Iran, Russia and Latin America. Then there are Asians from the Far East and Israeli Arabs, the latter group enjoying more personal freedoms in Israel than they would in any Arab state.

My experiences in Israel might seem surprising to the reader who hasn't been there – particularly given the predominance of reports casting the country as a villainous, apartheid state. There exists a peculiar unwillingness to accept good news from Israel, which contrasts with the way that paradigm-shifting reports on 'The hidden modernity of Tehran' are welcomed with open arms. When I attempted to include the scene that I had witnessed at the traffic lights in a magazine feature I wrote about the research trip to Israel, I had to go through an exasperating discussion with the commissioning editor. He didn't seem to know that Israeli Arabs existed and insisted that the scene I described couldn't have occurred. He'd never been to Israel but was quite sure that he was right and I was wrong.

He was in good company in his blissful ignorance. Within hours of my return from the trip, I received a call from a journalist acquaintance who asked me with genuine shock, 'What's all this about you going to Israel?' He said that a mutual journalist acquaintance of ours was 'absolutely disgusted' with me for going there and that he hoped I was 'going to put the boot in' when I wrote my articles. These were not close acquaintances; I hadn't even spoken to one of them for nearly nine years and it must have taken them some digging around to find my new telephone number. They obviously thought it was worth the trouble to have a dig at a writer who was friendly to Israel. Apparently the 'absolutely disgusted' man − a weekly columnist on a high-profile magazine − has since tried to get an article published that claims that Tony Blair murdered Yasser Arafat.

The editor of another magazine once told me I was not allowed to write that Yasser Arafat turned down Ehud Barak's offer at Camp David in 2000. I asked why and he replied, 'because of a need for balance'. I pointed out that nobody, including Arafat, has ever disputed that he rejected Barak's offer and the editor replied, 'Well, I don't know about that but you still can't write it.' The article in question was an 'opinion' piece and taking sides was the order of the day each edition in that column. Not if the article was about Israel, it seemed. Get this for hypocrisy, though: the same magazine had happily published articles accusing Israel of 'war crimes' and carried advertising accusing Israel of apartheid policies. Clearly, the need for balance is relative.

Not that there was much balance in the motion the National Union of Journalists passed in 2007 to boycott Israel. As a writer I felt shame and despair at this motion. Those emotions of shame and despair were not joined by shock, though, because much of the British media has long been absorbed by a blind hatred of Israel. Broadsheet newspapers print editorials that are so biased and distorted that Osama Bin Laden would probably blush at them and say, 'Steady on! We can't print that!' The BBC refuses to describe suicide bombers who blow up buses full of Israeli schoolchildren as 'terrorists' even though it has used that term to describe bombers in London, Iraq and Indonesia. One of its correspondents told a Hamas rally that he and his colleagues were 'waging the campaign shoulder to shoulder with the Palestinian people'.

Why did the NUJ choose Israel for a boycott? The country has an entirely free press. If the NUJ wanted to boycott a country then Russia, China, Zimbabwe and Pakistan would have been more sensible options, given their record on press freedom. The timing, too, was ridiculous. Shortly before the motion was passed, BBC journalist Alan Johnston was kidnapped by Palestinians in the Gaza Strip. So why did the NUJ respond to this by boycotting Israel?

The coverage of the Alan Johnston case was riddled with hypocrisy. Every day, the BBC devoted acres of space to the story. Yet the BBC largely ignored the plight of young Israeli soldiers who were kidnapped by Palestinians. Indeed, the BBC refuses to even use the term 'kidnap' in relation to the snatching of teenager Corporal Gilad Shalit, preferring to say he was 'captured'. I was in Israel during Johnston's captivity and had a conversation about his case with an Arab from the West Bank. He said, 'I'm surprised that they took someone from the BBC. Everyone knows the BBC is biased for the Palestinians. I bet they're not so for the Palestinians now, though!' When I told him that the BBC was just as pro-Palestinian as ever, he raised his eyes to the heavens. 'That's strange,' he said.

True. But then Auntie Beeb has long shown her true colours on the conflict. A 2007 leaked internal BBC memo written by a senior correspondent blamed Israel for all the woes of the Gaza Strip, despite the fact that Israel had withdrawn two years earlier from Gaza!

Hmm, what we need is a man who can effortlessly show these BBC buffoons just how hypocritical they are. Step forward and take a bow Benjamin Netanyahu, former Prime Minister of Israel and all-round hero of both myself and my co-author. He was interviewed on the BBC during the 2006 Hezbollah conflict and made mincemeat of his quizzer:

Interviewer: 'How come so many more Lebanese have been killed in this conflict than Israelis?'

Netanyahu: 'Are you sure that you want to start asking in that direction?'

Interviewer: 'Why not?'

Netanyahu: 'Because in World War Two more Germans were killed than British and Americans combined, but there is no doubt in anyone's mind that the war was caused by Germany's aggression. And in response to the German blitz on London, the British wiped out the entire city of Dresden, burning to death more German civilians than the number of people killed in Hiroshima.

'Moreover, I could remind you that, in 1944, when the RAF tried to bomb the Gestapo headquarters in Copenhagen, some of the bombs missed their target and fell on a Danish children's hospital, killing eighty-three little children.

'Perhaps you have another question?'

Perhaps indeed! Perhaps the academics who chose to boycott Israel at the same time as the NUJ might have asked themselves some questions too. In 2007, they voted to boycott Israeli academic institutions in a protest supposedly on behalf of the Palestinians.

Meanwhile, back in the real world a young Jordanian-Palestinian woman was graduating with a Master's degree from Ben Gurion University in Israel. Dana Rassas was trained by the Arava Institute for Environmental Studies at Kibbutz Ketura in the Negev, and then went on to study the Israeli water desalination programme at the Albert Katz International School for Desert Studies at Ben Gurion University. As a result of her studies in Israel, Rassas is now helping to solve Jordan's water problems. If the boycotters had their way, she'd never have had any of these chances.

To take a wider view, why is it that so many people who cling to the notion of human rights when considering the plight of the Palestinians couldn't give a hoot about other groups around the world like the Tibetans, the Kurds, the Armenians and the Chechens? Is it because these groups didn't have the fortune of being in dispute with Jewish people? Either way, it is indisputable that the incessant focus of the human rights movement on the actions of Israel has allowed genuinely horrific human rights abuses in other parts of the world to go unnoticed.

As we keep seeing, whatever it does Israel cannot win and so we end up returning to the graffiti seen by Amos Oz's father in Poland. First: go back to Palestine; then: get out of Palestine. Anti-Semitism has always been dominated by contradictions. The Jews have been attacked for being both communist schemers and capitalists plotting to take over the world. They can't stop sticking their noses into others' business yet they also must be attacked for keeping themselves to themselves. They were taunted for being too weak when the Germans tried to eliminate them from the face of the earth and are now slammed for being too strong when the Arabs try the same trick.

Ironically, for all the attention and criticism that Western hypocrites throw at Israel, the biggest questioners of the state and its actions are Israelis themselves. Israel's Supreme Court is a thorn in the side of the government and army and frequently overrules both. It regularly examines petitions brought by Palestinian people and rules in their favour. Many of its judgements have restricted the options open to the army and, in passing them, the Court has acknowledged that its rulings will cause Israeli loss of life, but insisted that such steps are needed in the interests of humanity.

When terrorist leaders who have arranged the slaughter of Israeli people are killed by the Israel Defence Force, there is no cheering in the street, as is seen among Palestinians when another school bus is blown up by a suicide bomber, a favourite tactic of theirs, for example in November 2000. Instead, commissions of inquiry are set up to examine whether the elimination of these men who wanted to murder their children was ethical and correct. On and on it goes, this relentless self-examination by a country that has faced abuse, distortion and calls for its destruction since the very minute it was established in 1948.

But then that's the thing about Israel: strong, plucky, moral, deeply self-critical yet determinedly happy and upbeat, it is everything the modern hypocrite is not. I love it.

CUBA
Chas Newkey-Burden

In my opinion, Israel is the fulcrum for more left-wing hypocrisy than any other country on the planet. Not far behind, though, is Cuba. Fidel Castro and Che Guevara are the poster boys of the modern hypocrite. No amount of crimes can be revealed to have been committed by these men that groovy lefties will not be willing to overlook as they don their Guevara and Cuba T-shirts and sip their commie cocktails.

The fact that these men represent so much of what the left is supposed to deplore never gets in the way of the party. Just take Castro's record on gay people. He persecuted gays and lesbians throughout the 1960s and 1970s, locking them up without trial in brutal labour camps. Some 'disappeared' while in the camps and were never seen again. Even after these camps were closed, young gay men were forced to undergo horrendous aversion therapy. Castro also boasted that 'in the country there are no homosexuals' – this was echoed by Iranian dictator Mahmoud Ahmadinejad in 2007 – and then tried to make that statement come true by ordering all gay 'scum' to leave Cuba during the 1980s.

People locked up in labour camps because of their sexuality – it's quite a thing to overlook, isn't it? However, in the twenty-first century the same people who look the other way when it comes to Castro's crimes are a lot more clear-eyed as they scream their opposition to the Guantanamo Bay camp. Strange, isn't it, that the same people who have nothing bad to say about people being locked up in Cuba for being gay are so angry when people are locked up in Cuba because they're suspected of plotting apocalyptic terrorism? Speaking of Guantanamo Bay, there was a nasty whiff of hypocrisy in the air when three inmates committed suicide there in 2006. A state-sponsored group in Saudi Arabia were the first out of the traps to protest and squeal about human rights. The fucking pot calling the kettle black, or what? And anyway, what's the problem? I'd much rather someone committed suicide quietly in a prison cell than noisily in the middle of Times Square or Piccadilly Circus, with a nuclear bomb strapped to their waist and a dream of millions of corpses in their head.

As for Che Guevara, what a nasty piece of work he was. He lined up political opponents against the wall and shot them, bragging that he 'didn't need' proof to execute anyone, becoming known as 'The butcher of La Cabana' in the process. He boasted that there was not 'a single discrepancy' between his views and those of his hero Mao Zedong. He begged President Khrushchev to nuke American cities and reasoned that, if such an act led to Cuba being attacked in revenge, then its people would die feeling 'completely happy and fulfilled'.

'What a hero,' shrieks the modern hypocrite. 'Quick! Get me a T-shirt with his face on it!' Indeed, one Guevara groupie paid £60,000 for a lock of his hero's hair. Turning rebellion into money, I believe they call it? But why do modern lefties so continually overlook the excesses of dictators and terrorists? Is it a series of coincidences or something more sinister? And why do the same people who attack the US for its Guantanamo Bay camp in Cuba idolise a man who executed opponents without trial on the same island?

Perhaps they believe that, in certain fights, certain struggles, it can be acceptable to play around with the rule book? If so, then surely the struggle against terrorists who want to nuke, poison, bomb or destroy us all via any other means that come to mind, is the one time that it is justified to put the Queensberry rules to one side? Surely this is a much more bloody and important fight than anything that Guevara was involved in?

GEORGE BUSH BASHERS
Chas Newkey-Burden

George W Bush is bad, right? Absolutely everything about him is evil. Whatever else we may disagree on, we can all agree that Bush is bad and therefore we are good. Right? That's about as high-minded as any discussion of Bush gets, which is ironic given that it is Bush who is supposed to be stupid and not his detractors. However, the Bush basher will immediately cover their ears if you try and point out another side to the man.

So never try and tell a modern hypocrite that George W Bush has been widely praised by leading aid workers for his radical and positive approach to poverty and famine in Africa. Don't waste your time informing them that, throughout his career, Bush has championed the rights of immigrants. Neither should you bother reminding them that, once he became president, Bush filled senior governmental positions with unprecedented numbers of brilliant, black politicians. They simply won't be listening.

It was Sir Bob Geldof who first flagged up Bush's brilliance on Africa. 'You'll think I'm off my trolley,' he said, 'but the Bush administration is the most radical – in a positive sense – in its approach to Africa, since Kennedy.' Sir Bob contrasted this to Europe's 'pathetic and appalling' response and

Clinton's record: 'he did fuck all'. Many aid charities have echoed his praise for Bush. Bono, too, has had many good things to say about him. None of this is good enough for your modern hypocrite, though. For them, Bush will always be the devil incarnate. Funny, isn't it, how people who contribute no more to the cause than buying a white wristband should feel so comfortable hurling abuse at a man who has done more than most on the planet to help Africa?

He has not just helped bring aid to impoverished Africans, he has also helped bring hope to those living under harsh regimes. In 2005, Egyptian president Hosni Mubarak jailed an opponent who was planning to challenge him in the presidential election. Bush pressured Mubarak – who prefers to run for the presidency unopposed – into releasing his opponent. When private pressure didn't work, the Bush administration made its disapproval public. Then Condoleezza Rice cancelled a planned trip to Egypt in protest, Mubarak relented and Dr Ayman Nour was released.

Not that any of this will stop his detractors from thinking Bush is racist. So it's hugely inconvenient for them to learn that in 1994 he passionately opposed a bill in California that would cut access to public services for illegal immigrants. He is actually a hero of many immigrants in America: for instance, his share of the Hispanic vote increased by 9 per cent during his first term as president.

So, no, it's not just Midwest Bible-bashers who voted for Bush. While we're on the religion issue, did you know that Bill Clinton publicly referred to Jesus Christ more times than Bush did? Bush averaged 4.7 times a year while Clinton averaged 5.1 annually. Similarly, during the 2004 presidential campaign, Democrat John Kerry made a campaign speech in a church in St Louis and used a biblical quote to attack Bush, who never campaigned in a church and never quoted from the scriptures. However, when Bush mentions faith he is bad, but when a Democrat mentions faith it's fine, almost groovy!

Intellectuals at English dinner parties have long enjoyed poking fun at Bush's mangling of the English language. He acknowledges his weakness in this regard but shrugs, 'You know, life goes on.' Or in other words, 'Let the European snobs sneer all they like, ordinary people in the US know and appreciate where I'm coming from.' But how they love sneering! They also like pointing to the controversy over his 2000 election victory. However, just as they attack him with allegations of foul play, they simultaneously overlook similar allegations made against the Democrats. Cheating is either wrong or it's not – it ill behoves us to condemn it only in some instances and not others.

Hypocrisy with a more chilling streak is found in those who like to suggest that Bush and Blair orchestrated 9/11 and 7/7. Yet, when it comes to the embarrassing lack of WMDs in Iraq, none of these conspiracy theorists stops to think that, if these men arranged terrorist outrages in their own cities, they might just have been able to stretch as far as fabricating evidence of WMDs in Baghdad. Likewise, the same people who say that Bush engineered 9/11 are also quick to point out how he sat frozen in shock in that classroom when he first learned of the atrocity. You can only imagine what the modern hypocrite's response to 9/11 would have been had they been in Bush's shoes. Probably something like, 'Quick! Give them what they want so they stop!'

There's sometimes a genuinely insane dimension to the anti-Bush bandwagon. At a gathering of world leaders at the United Nations in September 2005, Bush was seen passing a note to Condoleezza Rice. The contents of this note brought him fresh abuse from his detractors who used it as yet more confirmation that he's the most unpleasant man ever to have lived. And what was the content of this controversial note? It read, 'I think I may need a bathroom break? Is this possible?' A man who's been in meetings all day wants to make sure he follows the correct etiquette about using the bathroom. How sick!

Of course, for most Bush bashers there is the wider issue of anti-Americanism at stake. These are the people who so enjoy mocking Americans as overweight and American television as dumbed-down crap. Funny, then, that they still manage to be such passionate fans of Michael Moore, who carries a bit of weight himself and makes, in my opinion, the most simplistic documentaries imaginable.

Of course, there are things about Bush that aren't great: it would be silly to overlook his record on abortion and gay rights for a start. However, the truly silly ones are those who blindly bash Bush whatever he does or says. Has there ever been a less intelligent, less discriminating or more sheep like political movement than the anti-Bush bandwagon? It is one of the most hypocritical movements of all time, that's for sure.

ANTI-AMERICANISM
Chas Newkey-Burden

In April 2002, a lone gunman opened fire in a town hall in western Paris, killing eight people and injuring nineteen. The killer was of Yugoslav origin and his victims were French. So which country, if any, should get the blame for the killings? Perhaps French Presidential candidate Alain Madelin can help us. He described the shootings as an 'American-style by-product, we wished not to have in France.' Quoi?

Anti-Americanism has been around for so long that it is not a modern hypocrisy in itself. I recall that when my political awakening happened at the age of twelve, there were no end of demonstrations against military actions, executions and human rights abuses. But nearly all of them were about American military actions, American executions, American human rights abuses. America every time. It was as if the rest of the world – excepting perhaps South Africa – was a peaceful idyll, with everyone cycling up and down country lanes, waving at each other and petting small cuddly animals.

However, in the twenty-first century it has increased dramatically – one poll showed that 'favourable opinions' of America between 2000 and 2006 dropped from 83 per cent to 56 per cent in the UK – and so anti-Americanism forms a central plank of this book's topic. As one commentator put it, anti-Americanism has become a hobby in Europe. You don't need to be a keen historian to note that this hobby has become increasingly popular since the 9/11 attacks. One wonders what sort of person watched that carnage and decided to get angry not with the aggressors, but the victims.

But then one wonders a lot about what is going in the minds of anti-Americans. Much was made of how Palestinians on the streets of the West Bank cheered the 9/11 attacks. However, numerous reports surfaced of similar joy in Europe. A friend of mine rang me from a bar in Chelsea where he said all the customers were punching the air with joy as the Twin Towers collapsed. Rosemary Righter of *The Times* was asked by a friend that evening: 'Rosemary, isn't it marvellous to think that the arrogant bloody Americans have finally got it in the neck?'

These are not one-off, rare instances of feelings running high on a strange day. Christian Cox, a US citizen who moved to England, has talked to the BBC about the levels of hatred and fury she has encountered in recent years for the simple crime of being American. She had travelled much of the world, but it was only on moving to England that she experienced genuine vitriol and loathing, she said. Amid this loathing, she detected almost a joyfulness in people's hatred: 'It's as if they had been waiting to run into an American all day to let their feelings out.' She found she had to spell out to these 'intellectuals' that just because the President of the United States made decisions they did not agree with, that did not mean she had to be held responsible for it. She'll be having to tie their shoelaces next.

When one man started shouting obscenities at her and some friends, the row turned into a fight and she ended up with a black eye. She had shared her experiences on the BBC website. Reader comments were included at the bottom of the page. One comment suggested that she 'keep her voice down'. In the end, she took to pretending to be Canadian to stave off the abuse. Congratulations, guys, you've got visitors to our country feeling they have to pretend to have a different nationality. If only her experiences were rare. The American writer Carol Gould has told me of endless abuse she has experienced in London because of her American accent. This has included her being forced to leave a coffee shop because a man was calling her an 'American pig'. She is now considering leaving England, a country she finds unrecognisable to the one she arrived in decades ago.

Some would call that a victory for racism and bigotry, which is accurate but perplexing, given the supposed anti-racist credentials of left-wing anti-Americans. Because it is very strange that so many of those who would happily describe themselves as anti-racist are among the worst critics of America. These are the first to jump up and howl if any generalisation is made of a race or nationality elsewhere in the world, yet with America they are delighted to make the most sweeping of statements. Let's be honest: few of us in England know much about America beyond a few large cities, and many of our number are not even as clued-up as that. Yet more and more of us are willing to damn an entire nation and its people on so little evidence. Oh, the exhausting irony of it, then, when these damners are so quick to accuse the Middle Americans they have never met of being ignorant or arrogant! And where, one has to ask, is the respect of these anti-racists for the cultural melting pot that America represents?

We saw in the Israel essay the contradictory attacks that the Jewish people have faced throughout their history. A similar process applies to America. At once the country is derided for being in league with Israel and yet in the pocket of Saudi Arabia. Can both of these be true? Not that this is the only gymnastics America is supposedly capable of, according to its critics. Just like the Jews and Israel, America manages to be attacked on any number of contradictory fronts. Talk about damned if you do, damned if you don't. America is: decadent and immoral, yet conservative and stuffy. It is dominated by Christian rednecks, yet also run by a smart, metropolitan Jewish cabal. It is selfish and isolationist, yet rampaging and imperialistic. It is full of commercially driven consumers, yet it is dominated by an old-fashioned, outdated obsession with religion and morals.

Sounds like a lot of fun; I'd quite like to live there.

That said, this essay was written as I travelled round America in February 2008. As I travelled past the 'Welcome

Home' posters for US troops, and sat in the coffee shops where customers can send coffee to the troops in Afghanistan and Iraq, I noted a congruency between the way people benefit from these wars and their gratitude for the brave souls who are fighting them. Quite a contrast from England, where the soldiers are either viewed condescendingly as the lambs to the slaughter of 'bring home our boys', or as rampaging racists. Or perhaps the most saddening in a strange way, merely ignored as they fight to break up the terror camps where yours and my deaths are being plotted. Where Ms Cox encountered abuse and hostility in bars of England, I had a crystallising conversation in a US bar about anti-Americanism, and the hypocrisy thereof. A guy I was chatting with said, very simply, that he couldn't understand why Europeans felt they had such a right to complain about dark moments in the history of US foreign policy. 'Take a look in your own backyard,' he said. 'You guys let six million Jews die only a matter of decades ago.'

While not wishing to come across all 'I'm a traveller, not a tourist' on you, I must say that bumping into fellow Brits while in America is rarely a welcome moment for me. Whenever it happens, they seemed to be rolling their eyes at some aspect of American culture or practice. It's not like anyone forced them to be there. However, perhaps the most clear-cut moment of hypocrisy came when I frequently heard British people complain about the level of security at American airports. In the weeks after 9/11, the consensus in England was how naive Americans had been about airport security, particularly for internal flights. 'The security is hardly tighter than it is for train journeys in England,' they sneered. And then security gets tightened, so they moan about that.

We return to a theme mentioned earlier about Iraq: those who marched against America's war on terror simultaneously were benefiting from it. This war defends not just our right to be free to demonstrate in Trafalgar Square, but it also defends our right to live, against those who would happily explode dirty bombs in Trafalgar Square were they not being relentlessly monitored, tracked and killed. Every day we are not blown up by a dirty bomb, we are benefiting from the war on terror so the relentless criticism of America's foreign policy is not just hypocritical, but ungrateful.

In any case, in what way do British critics of American foreign policy believe that our foreign policy differs from America's? America fought in Iraq. Erm, so did we. America battled the Taliban and Al-Qaeda in Afghanistan. Oops! We did too! Washington backs Israel. So do we. They have nuclear weapons, and we've got a few of them as well. And so on. It's hard not to feel that a lot of anti-Americanism is merely a form of projection by its perpetrators.

The idea of spreading freedom and democracy has become a key sneering point of the modern hypocrite. It is an idea which has reached its peak in the early twenty-first century. I wonder what would go through the minds of those who lived through the darkest hours of the previous century, as various forms of fascism, tyranny and genocide threatened humanity, would feel if they discovered that the biggest evil in the minds of many in 2008 is the idea that a country might be trying to spread democracy. How spoilt are the anti-Americans.

Their targets are frequently bizarre. In the wake of 9/11, much was rightly made of the courage of the firemen who rushed into the Twin Towers as they burned. Quickly, this quite justified hero-worship began to be questioned by America's enemies, who began to snigger or sneer at the fact that Americans felt proud and sentimental towards brave men who walked to their deaths while trying to save their fellow citizens. On a more everyday level, Americans' omnipresent chorus of 'Have a nice day' has become another sneering-point for the nation's detractors. Me, I rather like it, but given what a miserable bunch the modern hypocrite is, I suppose it's no surprise that they are so offended by it.

A favoured chant of the anti-American is to talk of the country as an evil empire. That empire word gets me everytime. Just where is this empire? When the British and French had empires — the fact of which European anti-Americans conveniently overlook — they ruled a host of countries including India, Rhodesia, Ireland and Algeria. So would the millions of English and French that talk routinely of an American empire please get out a map and show us the long list of countries that America rules? Even when America has 'interfered' with the affairs of other regions, it has not sought to take over those regions. And it's not as if they lack the military ability to do so. Given America's enormous wealth, power and financial might, and the lack of tangible countries that would constitute an empire, one is kind of forced to accept that perhaps they really are not pursuing an empire.

On and on the hypocrisy goes. America-bashers gleefully live lifestyles that are dominated by American influence, both cultural and economic. Record shops in England do a roaring trade in America-bashing books, whilst happily cramming their shelves with American films and albums. Anti-Americans go to cinemas and restaurants and rock concerts that are influenced by the US of A. It's not just us Europeans, either: people in countries throughout the Middle East accept the hundreds of billions of dollars that America doles out in aid, and then burn the Stars and Stripes to show their gratitude. Then there was that 'Death To America' protestor, who was wearing a New York City jumper while calling for the destruction of the Great Satan.

More laughable still is that anti-Americans genuinely believe they are some sort of radical, downtrodden minority. Yet their number includes numerous top celebrities, royals, politicians and leading media players. Their argument that they are disenfranchised is laughable. They'd even have us believe that their voices are ignored by the 'dumbed-down, right-wing American media'. A pity, then, that numerous polls show that the majority of American journalists vote Democrat.

Speaking of elections, in 2008, everywhere you turned here in Britain, someone was expressing an opinion on the US Presidential race. Workplaces, pubs, bus stops and dinner parties were abuzz with discussion about the pros and cons of the various candidates as the primaries gathered pace. Even Facebook – that great stomping ground of the bored and attention-seeking – was not immune: British members used their 'status updates' not to express how hungover/excited/ bored they were, but to broadcast who they wanted the ultimate winner to be. Sentiments such as: 'Go Hillary!', or 'I'm backing Barack', or even 'Rudy's my man' were common-place on the social networking site.

Our own general election in 2005 provoked less excitement in these shores. The hypocrisy of this was not lost on me. In recent years we've made it a national pastime to throw up our hands in horror at the slightest suggestion of any American interference in our political scene, yet we still seem to believe that we're entitled, not to mention equipped, to take sides in the US Presidential race. One can only imagine the keep-your-noses-out horror that would erupt if at the next general election, Americans started encouraging us to vote for, say, David Cameron rather than Gordon Brown. So how come we can tell them what we think they should do?

I wonder too what was behind this surge in interest in this Presidential race. Granted, Britain – and indeed the rest of the world – has a vested interest in who takes the reigns of a country as powerful as America, so it could be argued that it's quite natural for us to keep an eye on the campaigns. But this argument only works up to a point, because America has long been a superpower, and yet most of us were content to let them get on with previous elections with minimal interest from over here. And if people really are only following proceedings because of the power of America, then why is there so little concern about the political scene in China, a nation with at least as much power as America? Those brave activists who protested at the Olympic torch ceremony in London in April 2008 are fighting a noble yet lonely battle, for criticism of China is still a minority sport in these shores.

I suspect a great deal of the growing interest in American politics over here is due to the boredom and apathy with which we regard our own political scene. Let's be honest: the battles between Clinton, Obama, McCain and the rest get the blood pumping far more than Gordon Brown, David Cameron and what's-his-name ever will. Another aspect of British attitudes to the 2008 Presidential race that was interesting was how those on the left who are ever ready to criticise America had not a word of praise for the fact that a great black man was vying with a smart woman for the Democratic nomination. This put our white, male, Etonian-dominated political system to a bit of shame, and yet anti-Americans managed to miss this glaring fact. Likewise, the thorough-ness of the electoral system in America is oft painted as thoroughly confusing by the country's critics. That's one way of looking at. Another way would be to say it's thoroughly democratic.

A final irony: many of those who followed the American elections with such interest from these shores are the same people who have bemoaned so bitterly the growing influence of America in this country. How amusing, then, that as they became more interested in the American elections than they are with anything going on in Westminster, they inadvertently confirmed a thesis that had been coined by perhaps their biggest nemesis, and one they had resisted and denied for so long: that we're all American now.

Amen, I say.

And another thing . . .

An aspect of American life that draws particular scorn from the modern hypocrite is the death penalty. Here's where the 'man/woman of the people' halos of many liberals well and truly falls off their deluded heads. Any opinion poll you care to name shows that the majority of people want capital punishment introduced in Britain. Yet the modern hypocrite believes that this groundswell of opinion should be ignored, in favour of the wishes of a small band of intellectuals who oppose its use even for murder or sex crimes where forensic evidence has removed all doubt. Could it be, one wonders, that it is not the supposed 'inhumanity' of America's use of the death penalty that really enrages the modern hypocrite, but rather the fact that over there, the people's wishes are listened to, and that the, ahem, minority intellectual elite are ignored?

CATHOLIC HYPOCRISY
Julie Burchill

In March 2008, the Vatican updated its original list of Seven
Deadly Sins – pride, envy, gluttony, lust, anger, greed and
sloth – with a new set of naughty no-nos whose breaching
would cause any Catholic to suffer ceaseless punishment in
Hell.

Well, they say if you're going to tell a lie make it a big one,
and in a similar manner to the quite ludicrous claims that
pride, lust and greed, for starters, are quite alien to the
Catholic Church, I couldn't resist a cheeky Protestant chuckle
when I read in the *Daily Mail* that one of the modern sins is
'causing poverty and accumulating excessive wealth at the
expense of the common good of society'. Pot, kettle,
black = hypocrite!

Others include drug use, pollution and mucking about with
embryos. See anything missing there? Yep, that would be the
sexual abuse of children – a sin which in recent years has
become as synonymous with the Catholic Church as married
vicars running off with one of the ladies who arranges the
church flowers has with the Anglican faith.

How brazen is it of them to weep over scientists interfering
with foetuses when, once that foetus becomes a child, any
number of evil liberties may be taken with it while the Church
looks the other way? Suffer little children indeed!

Take jolly old Ireland, just across the bay. When writing on
the black art that is rank hypocrisy, it would be remiss of me
to ignore the extraordinary contribution of those who, since
1922, purport to represent the Irish Catholic people in Ireland
and abroad. One of the first acts of the new independent Irish

government after 1922 was the closing of the only independent teacher-training college in Dublin – thus assuring Catholic domination of education in the State sector for more than sixty years in the curiously named Free State.

From the start, many politicians in the Free State realised that power didn't just come through the barrel of a gun – it could just as easily be had through the patronage of the Catholic Church. This led to 'understandings' on many levels – 'family life', for instance, was the preserve of the Church, and the 1937 constitution recognised 'the special position of the Catholic Church' in Ireland. This led to tragic consequences for tens of thousands of innocent people – mostly children who were illegally locked up for substantial periods in the creepily named 'Industrial Schools', invariably run by nuns and 'Christian brothers'. Schools in name only, their small inmates were deliberately denied access to anything more than the absolute statutory minimum in education and many were even denied that much – ignorance for these children being preferred by their captors, as it rendered them more malleable and vulnerable to massive sexual and physical abuse, and also useful as free labour to help line the Church's already groaning pockets, as in the case of the notorious Magdalene laundries, which existed until the 1970s, the very last one closing in the 1990s. Girls were placed here by their fathers for the 'sin' of being single mothers, rape victims or simply flirts; with typical hypocrisy, the agents of the Church then did their very best to actually turn them into 'fallen women'. The Vatican was furious when, in 2003, the film *The Magdalene Sisters* was released to applause and awards, and had the – again typically hypocritical, after all the terrible anti-Semitism, both in theory and practice, of the Catholic Church, especially during the Second World War and the

Holocaust – nerve to denounce anti-Catholicism as 'the anti-Semitism of the Left'. (As if the modern left were not itself filthy with anti-Semitism, as demonstrated elsewhere in this book.)

In post-British-ruled theocratic Ireland, the incredibly twisted situation existed where children were brought before the courts on application by a parent – usually the father with a claim against a disobedient wife, or a wife who had left him and gone abroad, normally to the UK, to escape his violent behaviour. Basically, it was an act of sheer spite on the part of the parent, hypocritically masquerading as concern for their children's moral welfare – and only a country so mired in religious hypocrisy could have perpetuated it for so long.

A child in such circumstances could then be committed for as long as sixteen years, unless or until the absent wife and mother returned to her husband and both parents made joint petition for the child's release. Of course, in the Free State divorce was illegal, as was contraception of any kind, so this nasty piece of immoral blackmail was created to keep women firmly in their place; she could be controlled through her children, or so went the thinking.

Some of the children locked up came from families that couldn't cope due to poverty – which flourished among the people as the wealth of the Church grew – and some were genuine orphans; so these two categories of infant were only punished by the Free State for being poor, or for being without parents! But what passed for 'social policy' in the country was the preserve of the Church, and the convoluted reasoning behind locking these children up was that the Church could take the place of the parents – this from people who had taken vows of celibacy and renounced married life for themselves!

A curious State indeed where pederasts became surrogate parents to tens of thousands of children who generally had mothers and fathers to whom they were returned at the age of sixteen, damaged to various degrees after many years of abuse. In exchange for these grotesque services, the State provided the Catholic Church with money, land and property, and of course an enormous army of vulnerable children to work on the land and anything else their clerical captors desired. The arrangement was, in short, diabolical and anti-family, and had everything to do with the State endowing religion – an act which was in itself specifically in violation of the all-important Constitution.

At the largest Industrial School in Ireland, Artane in North Dublin, where up to 800 boys were locked up in the 1950s under the tender mercies of the Christian Brothers, the children worked from morning to night in workshops producing goods to be sold in the picturesque city centre – many, no doubt, to tourists, oohing and aahing over the unspoilt, family-orientated values of the Emerald Isle compared to the rest of the ever-changing English-speaking nasty modern world! No Protestant work ethic here, you can just imagine them cooing, where the twinkly-eyed old priests always had time to stop and smell the Guinness, and the obedient children trotted obediently after their loving parents into Mass of a Sunday . . .

No – but what there was was the very Catholic work ethic of the time and place, where, behind the picture-postcard scenes, forced child labour worked in all seasons on Artane's 300-acre farm, supplying eggs to hotels, hospitals and dairies throughout the country; the reward for these small slaves being a single boiled egg a year – at Easter. Such activities handsomely filled the troughs of the Church's various orders, handsomely supplementing the weekly State capitation fees paid for each child locked up.

To further advance the grossly hypocritical view Ireland likes to push of itself as an enchanted island full of song and joy, Artane had a world-famous boy band which travelled throughout Ireland, the UK and the USA giving public concerts which raised a great deal of money – often for other religious-run 'normal' schools for the children of the middle classes, which might need a new library or science laboratory.

But it apparently never occurred to the Christian Brothers to organise a concert in aid of a library for Artane itself; imagine that, a 'school' which lasted for ninety-nine years without a library, under the management of Ireland's 'premier teaching order' – the 'Christian Brothers'.

What Artane did have, however, was its own graveyard, which was fortunate as during its 99-year existence over 240 boys died there. Not every school can boast such an unusual feature.

Asked by the local Archbishop in 1962 to compile a secret report on conditions at Artane, the chaplain issued a report which was suppressed until August 2007. Then, under pressure from Irish SOCA, the current Archbishop of Dublin released the fourteen-page Moore Report of 1962 which revealed the shocking level of violence and cruelty endured by the long-suffering children of Artane.

'Overcoats are not supplied except where a boy can pay £3 or £4 in advance, which must come from his own pocket. It is pathetic to watch hundreds of boys walking the roads of the district on Sunday mornings even in deep winter without overcoats.'

There were also, of course, graphic accounts of savage beatings which the chaplain had personally witnessed, but of particular note perhaps is the passage which refers to the resounding failure the Christian Brothers were when it came to religious instruction.

'Religion seems to make little or no impression on the majority of the boys. With many ex-pupils, the practice of their faith is a burden to be shunned, and they associate their religious training with repression. Indeed, many of the problems I encounter are quite alarming.'

A Catholic religious order, established under Papal licence and with permission from the local Archdiocese, turning the young away from religion while enjoying both Church and State patronage! Little wonder that the reaction of the Christian Brothers to the release of the report was outrageously illogical, attacking the Archbishop's decision to release the report as 'unconscionable' – appearing not to grasp that it was their vile behaviour towards generations of innocent children that was truly unconscionable; not to mention reeking of hypocrisy.

In May 1999, the Irish Prime Minister Bertie Ahern issued an apology to the past inmates of the Industrial Schools for what he called 'our failure to detect their pain', at the same time setting up a Commission of Inquiry under the chairmanship of a High Court judge – Ms Justice Mary Laffoy. Sadly, Justice Laffoy resigned in August 2003, claiming 'lack of co-operation' from the government. After nine years' delay and millions of euros in legal costs, the inquiry goes on and has yet to publish its final report.

In England, the Ahern apology was received by the Irish Centres – traditionally run by one of the most abusive Catholic religious orders (The Oblates of Mary Immaculate) – as a golden opportunity to cash in on the victims and within months large sums of money from the Irish government were pouring into the centres to finance many an 'outreach' initiative. Financial assistance continues to this day, although the majority of the survivors want nothing whatsoever to do with Irish Centres, because there really can't be anything more despicable – not to mention hypocritical! – than an abuser cashing in the suffering of his victims, can there?

ICAP (Immigrant Counselling and Psychotherapy) was specifically set up post-apology to target the victims of Industrial Schools living in the UK, the director being a nun of the Loretto Order. Funding for ICAP is paid each year by the Irish Government Department of Health and Children; some things never change, least of all Catholic hypocrisy.

THE COST OF FAME

Hollywood Hypocrites; Guilty Pleasures; Hypocritical Comedians; Reality Talent Shows, Sour-Faced Haters of; Fame-Dissing Famous; Amy Winehouse Knockers; Graffiti and the Guardianista; Posh Confessionals Vs Common Kiss and Tells

HOLLYWOOD HYPOCRITES
Julie Burchill

It shouldn't come as any surprise that those who choose acting as a profession are phonies who live in a fantasy world. What is surprising is how many of them are blissfully unaware of it. It has a modern slant, too. The current-day Hollywood is populated by bigger hypocrites than ever.

Legends from Ava Gardner to Richard Burton would routinely get drunk with the journalists sent to write about them, and in the process casually pour contempt on their talent, the industry and, most deliciously of all, the whole myth of acting as an art. Richard Burton once claimed that all actors were gay and only went into showbiz so they could wear make-up every day without being beaten up.

How impossible it is to imagine the 'real' film stars of today doing this! When Oscar Wilde said that being natural is surely the biggest pose of all, he must have foreseen the current crop of big-screen luvvies, those po-faced, 'fiercely private', paparazzi-hating ponces who have chosen to expose themselves on screens the size of churches – often naked! – in return for vast amounts of money from paying strangers. And then act outraged when they find people looking! These attacks of the vapours invariably come across as about as justifiable as a stripper getting upset when people expect her to take her clothes off, and you can ALMOST see why star-stalkers sincerely believe that they're married to their favourite flesh-flashing star. I mean, if someone shows you their vagina, doesn't it at least mean they sort of fancy you? Either that or they're a random flasher, in which case THEY'RE the nutter and you're obviously in the clear. Just keep telling that to the judge!

(It isn't hard to imagine some Hollywood actresses looking with amazed disdain at any of the numerous pap shots of young starlets getting out of cars commando and shuddering 'Uck! Disgusting! Why would anyone want to do that unless it was in front of the paying public? Girls today!' Like a prostitute I knew who looked down on sexually generous, unpaid girls as sluts, 'because they give it away'!)

While ceaselessly lying to themselves and the public about how the process of acting – i.e. pretending to be someone else, by reciting words yet another someone else has written – is all about 'honesty', modern actors never dare to face the one stark, simple truth about the way they have chosen to make a living. Which is that they have never grown out of the Look at me! stage of childhood; they want attention, pure and simple, more than they want anything else in life, including regular one-to-one human relationships, and this desire embarrasses them so much in their rare lucid moments that they overcompensate by endlessly and ludicrously insisting on how 'private' they essentially are. They're not doing this for themselves, you know! – they're doing it for mankind! For all those ungrateful punters who want a piece of them – the sad bastards! They're very private people – THAT'S

WHY THEY SHOW THEIR PRIVATES! See what a logical progression that is?

The pain actors willingly submit to, the bravery they display, the sacrifices they make – JUST FOR US! – fair makes the civilian mind boggle with sheer molten awe. Why, they make nurses, firemen and volunteers in leper colonies – ALL OF THEM EVER, ALL ROLLED TOGETHER! – look like the Hilton sisters on a spring-break spree! SO WHY WON'T WE JUST STOP LOOKING AT THEM! Of course, when we do, and they cease to be box office, they move on to reality shows, finding yet another way of getting themselves in our faces. The sad, strange fact is that it is stars who stalk civilians far more often than civilians stalk stars. So who's the weirdo here?

So shameful do the stars find this uncomfortable truth – that they need our attention more than we need their presence; that we can effortlessly replace them with another screen idol but they can never replace the mass love of an audience – that they will go to any lengths to obscure it. They do this by constructing elaborate 'don't care' personae that are designed to draw the eye of the paying public away from the fact that they care about being admired by strangers more than anything else in the world.

Considering how liberal Hollywood likes to consider itself, the gender divide between the roles that actors and actresses assume in order to appear 'real' is far more extreme and traditional than it is in real, despised life. Female film stars, no matter how much they sneer at the alleged redneck sexism of Republican governments, drool on about full-time mother-hood and the supreme importance of 'family' – while churning out film after film, back to back, and enjoying divorce after divorce after sleeping with their latest co-star – in a way that would have a Surrendered Wife from the Bible Belt retching. One does not need to be a card-carrying Bush-baby to see the irony in the searing image of the black, single, career woman Condoleezza Rice, so dignified and serene in her eternal black trouser suits, stepping down from the plane, head boldly uncovered in yet another gynophobic Muslim country, as she goes about the serious business of seeking peace with justice where generations of white men have failed, compared to that of the white film stars sloppily keening for a 'peace' that consists solely of the West shirking its responsibilities and letting dark-skinned people murder each other in their millions. (It's called isolationism, STUPID, and its reputation died with Munich in 1938.)

Then there are those stars who are forever banging on about their loathing of materialism, while nursing an addiction to appearing in commercials for wanky luxury goods. As if they were not making enough money already, of course, often in a series of films that treat the most toe-curling depictions of violence as a sexy, groovy giggle. Interestingly, when Hollywood actresses have a chance to lend their famous names to a genuine struggle, they are conspicuous by their absence. At the 2004 abortion rights march on Washington, the only famous names were Ashley Judd, Lynda Carter, Whoopi Goldberg, Kathleen Turner and Cybill Shepherd – a Southern glamour gal turned tough, cool cookie in the manner of the immortal Ava. Yet, if we take into consideration that one in three American women has had an abortion, how much higher must the figure be among actresses? No disrespect (heh heh) but these broads as a breed are so fanatically ambitious – despite all the mealy-mouthed mummery – that it would hardly come as a shock to find out that the rate for abortion among working actresses is one in two, if not higher. But obviously standing up for the abortion rights of ordinary women – mere 'civilians' – would jar with their rather theatrical love of motherhood and family.

So, as it turned out, doing something that would actually earn them the anger of the Middle American narrow-minded they profess to despise is totally beyond the posturing cretins.

Female film stars do Domestic Goddess when they want to pass as 'real people'; male film stars go to the other extreme and do Wild Untamed Beast. But, rather pathetically, the Hollywood tough guy is invariably some sort of pampered brat whose mum's a casting agent/drama coach and/or whose dad's a dentist.

Of course, hypocrites worldwide have had a field day with the Iraq war. Hollywood is full of play-acting opponents of the heroic Anglo-American unseating of Saddam who seem to have difficulty relating personal behaviour to political posturing. These ceaseless celebrity critics of the West's intervention against tyranny sum up well the ill-sorted mindset of those self-proclaimed freedom lovers who paradoxically believe that fascist dictators should be allowed to murder as many of 'their own' people as they wish, while the rest of the world looks the other way. And, like, EVERYTHING IS EVERYTHING – AND BUSH IS TO BLAME!

Their other favourite hobby horse is the environment, and some of their number have tried to build a connection between global warming and Iraq – namely, why are we fighting in Iraq and not against global warming? Ironically, there is a connection but not necessarily the one they thought of. There has been a link between ecological damage and Iraq. But that damage was caused by Iraq itself, after that country invaded and massacred its innocent fellow Muslims in ever-peaceful Kuwait in 1990. When Western forces led by the US intervened and forced them to retreat in 1991, the Iraqi army decided to do all the damage it could, setting fire to Kuwait's vast oil fields and charmingly placing landmines around them so that fire-fighting crews could not move in. The fires burned for months, polluting soil and air, causing untold environmental damage to the region.

It was during this first intervention against the Ba'athist Nazis that the West stupidly held back from going all the way and unseating Saddam, for fear of offending 'Muslim pride'. What a strange, sad pride it is, that can better stand thousands of Muslims being murdered by a Muslim dictator than see them live, liberated from him by the Infidel! But, of course, Islamic pride is not alone here; the Hollywood antiwar hypocrites would prefer it if their golden boy was still there today – unmolested by the heavy hand of democracy – raping and torturing and murdering as the fancy took him.

And, let's not beat around the bush here: Saddam and his chums would cut the clits off the female Hollywood hypocrites soon as look at them. Perhaps these celebs should remember that in America, which according to them is ruled by a redneck Christian theocracy, their prime-time antagonism to the Bush administration has been rewarded with all the attention and riches their needy, greedy souls could desire.

It's fascinating watching Hollywood try to grapple with these issues. It's like watching parrots blithely debating the case in favour of animal experimentation, secure in their belief that they will never be used. And so grotesquely fascinating to see these people, who presumably believe in the brotherhood of man and claim to loathe the way that the affluent white West takes its comfort for granted while turning its back on the wretched of the earth, talk in such stark, selfish terms – 'What did Iraq do to us?' Well, if you mean what did

Saddam's Iraq do to rich white American film stars, not an awful lot. But, to thousands upon thousands of innocent Iraqis, torture, murder and genocide, for a start. And every one of the innocent victims of the Ba'athist terror was someone's child, someone's sister or brother, someone's mother or father. Someone worth fighting for. Civilians.

And civilians is, of course, what actors call non-actors. How perfectly, precisely, supremely hypocritical that these pampered, preening, lily-livered play-actors should use this word about people who are the very thing they're not, be they soldiers or servants – real.

GUILTY PLEASURES

Chas Newkey-Burden

How many dark secrets have you got in your CD, book and DVD collections? You know, those albums, novels and films that you love, but would simply die of embarrassment were anyone to discover them. I believe they call them 'guilty pleasures'. The idea of a 'guilty pleasure' is an unsettling one. What sort of beast feels guilt about pleasure? If we're going to start mixing up those two emotions, we might as well lie down and succumb to the forces of fundamentalism that would gleefully have us all shackled and flogged the moment we smile, dance or show any spontaneous joy.

It's also a hypocritical trend because if you have a guilty pleasure that suggests that you secretly own CDs, books or films that you would condemn others for enjoying.

I suppose it's because I so love pop that I take such umbrage at the idea of the guilty pleasure. After all, it's normally some of my favourite people – Britney, Robbie,

Leona, S Club 7, McFly – who are listed as musical guilty pleasures. Me, I've no shame at all over my love of their work and would only be ashamed if I started to prefer the 'credible' sounds of greying old rockers and their twenty-minute guitar solos, or woman-hating rappers, over the fun of McFly's 'Five Colours In Her Hair' or S Club's 'Don't Stop Movin''.

I wonder how dark a place someone must be in when they become embarrassed to savour the pure joy of the three-minute pop song. Weirder still are those who seek a 'credible way' to enjoy pop: they listen to the early-career, three-minute classics of the Kinks, or the Jam or the early Beatles, thus reasoning that pop is OK as long as the artist performing it is currently old enough to be a grandfather, rather than some lively youngster, as nature intended.

I will be forever suspicious of anyone who, as they grow older, decides that the joy of pop is something to be ashamed of. Those who genuinely do not enjoy it might be humourless but they are at least consistent. Worst of the lot are those hypocrites who sneer at others for openly liking pop, but secretly lap up plenty of that music behind closed doors. Creeps.

The televisual equivalent of this is the 'intellectual' reality television fan. These are the sorts who will avidly watch *Big Brother* and *The X Factor* but then feel guilty about it. As penance, they will then try and become 'intellectual' about the whole thing by identifying which parts of the show have been edited or merely by tirelessly slagging off the producers of the very shows they cannot stop watching. The forum at Digital Spy has had plenty such discussions down the years but the broadsheet newspapers are not adverse either to a bit of 'ironic' appreciation of reality television.

The guilty pleasure is like puberty: fine when you're a

moody, wannabe-intellectual teenager, but any later than that it's just disturbing.

HYPOCRITICAL COMEDIANS

Chas Newkey-Burden

Double entendres have always been a popular feature of comedy, but double standards are also increasingly all the rage among that bunch. Supposedly the realm of right-on, liberal values, the modern comedy world is in reality dominated by some of the most boorish, sexist men you could ever hope not to meet. Some of the most hypocritical, too.

One of the greatest woes of my life is the amount of time I've wasted watching the panel show *QI*, a show that regularly lays bare the horrible hypocrisy of modern comedy. Stephen Fry presides over this supposedly witty show in one of the most sombre studios in television history. A tangible air of regret hangs over the whole affair. After all, who wants to engage in anything that is 'quite interesting'? What's wrong with very interesting?

Given that many of the regulars on *QI* built their careers on being 'right-on' and 'alternative', it is surprising how comfortable they are with the almost entirely male, white panel policy on *QI*. Occasionally a woman is allowed into this Oxbridge-dominated realm, but everyone seems more comfortable when it's just guys. Apparently the concern is that women might 'freeze up' on screen! And in between trying to out-clever each other, they occasionally attempt humour, including, one week, a joke about Anne Frank. Let's leave aside the question of what topics, if any, are 'off limits' for humour. That debate is irrelevant here because the real issue is: what sort of person would want to make a joke about her? The sort of loser that goes on *QI*, clearly!

In recent times, more than one male comedian has taken to reading out excerpts from Jodie Marsh's autobiography for laughs. That's what I really resent about stale old male comedians – they make me defend Jodie Marsh of all people. Talk about a weak target! If they're so frustrated, why not just have a wank?

I would take Jodie any day of the week over any of the sexually frustrated male comedians who so resent their inability to get a piece of the beauty of young women that they snigger at it. Forget quite interesting; I've long thought that it would be very interesting if one week on that show the contestants were asked, 'What does having sex with another human being actually feel like?'

However, the most hypocritical moment connected with a BBC comedy show came during a meeting discussing *Room 101*. BBC executives at a corporation seminar were asked to rule on how they would react if Sacha Baron Cohen was a guest on the programme and wanted to consign to Room 101 the following: some kosher food, the Archbishop of Canterbury, a Bible and the Koran. The almost unanimous response was that all the objects could be thrown into the bin, except the Koran, for fear of offending Muslims.

How patronising is that to Muslims? They are effectively saying: Christians and Jews are big enough to take criticism but Muslims are not. When will these people realise that by mollycoddling Muslims in this way they are not avoiding Islamophobia, they are actually committing it and in a most condescending way? And how does BBC2 reconcile jokes about Anne Frank being acceptable but jokes about the Koran not being so? It's hypocrisy and it smells horrible.

Just in passing, respect to Rowan Atkinson who recognised that government attempts to make it illegal to joke about religions would not help Muslims. 'I appreciate this measure is an attempt to provide comfort and protection to them,' he said. 'But unfortunately it is a wholly inappropriate response far more likely to promote tension between communities than tolerance.'

However, most comedians remain happy to hop around any number of double standards when it comes to targets for their humour. A related double standard can be seen in the relentless, tidal wave of abuse that comedians direct at George W Bush and, increasingly, at America in general. Their right-on, anti-racist credentials would be so much more admirable if they didn't chuck them out of the window the moment it comes to America. When they describe all Americans as dumb and fat they're guaranteed a hearty cheer from indignant British audiences. Imagine the reaction they'd get if they tried to use similarly ridiculous stereotypes about people from Pakistan or Africa? Not that their dislike of America stops any of these comedy fans from enjoying brilliant American humour like *Frasier*, *Seinfeld* and *Friends*. While I'm about it, what is it with this idea that Americans 'don't get irony'? Have the people who say this never watched American comedies, which are rammed full of irony?

This is, after all, the generation of comedians who boasted that they were 'different', that they were 'alternative' indeed. They vowed to sweep away the old-school northern com-edians – it's always 'northern', but where do they think Jim Davidson came from? – and shake up the Establishment. The result was all too predictable: they now park their fat backsides on the television schedules at every opportunity. I rarely have a problem with anyone 'selling out' as long as I want to buy what they have, and I don't want most of what this lot are flogging.

Unsettling as all the hypocrisy is, the worst of it was seen when Chris Langham went to court in 2006. As we've seen, when sad old male rock stars lust over under-age girls either on the internet or in real life, there are no end of sad old male rock fans who will happily overlook it in a way they – quite rightly – never would if under-age boys had been the victim of the wandering rock stars' sticky fingers. The picture is scarcely less murky or hypocritical in comedy, as Langham's case showed. As soon as Langham was accused of various offences, comedy fans were quick to rally round and support their hero.

'Isn't it disgusting how his name is being dragged through the mud before anything has been proven?' they whined. Since when has the world of comedy ever cared about the concept of 'innocent until proven guilty'? The moment any politician or church leader is accused of doing anything wrong, the jokes are flying around the comedy circuit. However, when one of their heroes is in the spotlight, they suddenly go all protective and proper on us.

Not that it was merely a case of 'innocent until proven guilty' because, even once convicted, Langham had his defenders in comedy circles. Poor man, they said, his career is over. These men – they were all, as far as I could tell, men – had the breathtaking cheek to suggest that his crimes were in fact 'victimless'. Remember, he was convicted of fifteen charges of downloading child pornography including a video entitled *Kiddy* – featuring an eleven-year-old – and another video that featured an eight-year-old girl being sexually brutalised for fifteen minutes.

Victimless? Don't make me laugh.

And another thing . . .

The hypocrisy of the *Have I Got News For You* team was rarely more stark than in the wake of the disastrous fires in California in 2007. Hislop, Merton and the gang never sniggered at the earthquake that hit Pakistan – and neither should they have done. However, they couldn't stop making jokes about California. To them, the thousands of homes lost, the hundreds of thousands of people evacuated, were reasons for joy and laughter because they were American homes and American people.

REALITY TALENT SHOWS, SOUR-FACED HATERS OF
Julie Burchill

Whenever some new poll says that kids today want to be famous when they grow up, you can bet your life that some worry wart will moan, 'Ooo, why don't they want to be worthwhile things – like nurses or teachers?'

Funnily enough it's never people who actually do worthwhile jobs, like nurses or teachers, who put the damper on youngsters' perfectly understandable ambitions to have easy, rewarding careers in entertainment. It's journalists, who presumably didn't feel up to doing worthwhile jobs like being nurses or teachers, but reckoned they'd leave that to some other poor sucker who, unlike them, wasn't allergic to hard work and low pay. And would rather churn out yet ANOTHER piece comparing TV talent shows to Christians being thrown to the lions and defeated gladiators waiting for their death sentence under the cruel regime of Ancient Rome.

Don't know about you, but if a person can compare a voluntary talent show with the butchering of innocent human beings, I sort of feel that it's them who've lost their moral compass rather than Cowell and Co.

Oh, and other entertainers worry about these shows, too. As ever, there seems to be no end to the number of two-faced freaks willing to broadcast the hypocrite's Hippocratic Oath: 'Don't do as I do – do as I say!' It's easy to pity these – normally menopausal – moaners, if not to excuse them; popular music was always meant to be a young blood's business, and it must make the mask in the mirror look even more haggard if one can see the likes of young, lovely, talented Leona Lewis looking over one's shoulder. But that doesn't excuse such breathtaking mean-mindedness. Could it be that showbiz critics of reality television know that if they were to enter the type of show that Leona Lewis recently won, their talent wouldn't get them past the audition stage?

All popular music is 'manufactured' – that is, put together with an eye to the main chance at every stage of the process, from the first pop-paper personal column shout-out that puts 'credible' acts on the road to stardom, to the studio tricks used to beef up weak and reedy voices. Allegedly 'real' bands from the Beatles to the Sex Pistols had hapless founder members weeded out by silver-tongued Svengalis – and were all the better for it, because inauthenticity is in itself a prerequisite for the putative perfection of the modern sound. If you want authenticity, watch some morris dancing; if you want to laugh and cry, watch a reality TV talent show.

Oh, and in a direct contradiction of the idea that TV talent shows promote ambition without willingness to work, it was reported in the *Evening Standard* in August 2007 that 'the popularity of shows like *The X Factor* has led to an explosion of interest in acting and singing lessons at school. GSCE results are expected to show another surge in entries for music and drama.' In 2006, nearly 61,000 GCSE students took music – more than 23 per cent up since the year 2000. Said the very pleasant and astute-sounding Mr Steve Sinnott, leader of the National Union of Teachers, 'Music and drama are huge earners for this country and the growth in talent shows on TV has clearly spurred young people on.'

What a shame that the alleged natural-born 'stars' who criticise reality TV shows did not display the same eagerness to learn their craft at an early age as the *X Factor* generation has! For, if they had, they might not have had to construct their careers on an aural – and often, sadly, visual – combination of stalking and stripping. These are singers who behave like very strange creatures indeed; like lap dancers who leer at their punters, and have more interest in showing their nakedness than the paying public has in viewing it, peeling away layers of personality and clothing to keep us interested, then bleating that we made them do it when all they wanted was to be private people! Hypocrites, every one – and not even hypocrites who can hold a tune.

And another thing . . .

Wasn't there something patronising about BBC1's *Any Dream Will Do* when contestant Rob McVeigh was constantly referred to as 'Rob The Builder'? Andrew Lloyd Webber drooled, 'The thought of a builder on the West End stage is just delicious.' However, after a few weeks, the panel seemed to get bored with their bit of rough and slagged him off until the public voted him off. Likewise, it was Freddie Mercury who said he wanted to bring ballet to the working classes and in *Billy Eliott: The Musical* has his dream come true? Not at £59.50 for a seat in the stalls it hasn't!

FAME-DISSING FAMOUS
Julie Burchill

I almost choke on my popcorn when I hear film stars who walk on red carpets as much as the rest of us do on zebra crossings dissing youngsters who crave fame. Having secured and learned to love the trappings of fame, they try and kick the ladder away. Fact is, famous people say fame stinks because they love it so – like a secret restaurant or holiday island that they don't want the hoi polloi to get their grubby paws on. They love the fact that our society runs on parallel lines, with two different systems: capitalism, red in tooth and claw, for the poor and anonymous, and socialism for the rich and famous.

When you're a star, everything is free; for example, see the rise of the hideously named 'goody bags' that are now pressed on celebrities each time they attend the opening of an envelope. At the Oscars, gifts easily total one hundred thousand dollars per person, and over the years have contained everything from forty-thousand-dollar watches to holidays in Tahiti – all this just for turning up at a party, smiling for the camera and downing free booze!

Naturally the idea of losing all these perks – not to mention the main business of being paid more in a week to sing/play-act/dress up and walk along a catwalk than a nurse or teacher is paid in a year – is absolutely horrific to the rich and famous. Naturally they are protective of their astounding level of privilege. So they pile on the agony, talking up the 'stress' and 'pressure' of being paid millions to do very little apart from show off in one form or another, at any opportunity. And, in a thoroughly spiteful, mean-spirited and underhand attempt to ring the bell as soon as they're on the bus, they ceaselessly diss the bright, talented youngsters from TV talent shows. When all else fails, they enter rehab – 'See how fame has made me suffer! So stay in that McJob, kids, and don't try to follow me up the greasy pole!'

Celebrities try to foster the myth that fame is something that descends on individuals out of the blue, with no encouragement, blighting innocent lives; even Z-list personalities come out with astoundingly self-pitying statements about how fame has ruined their lives, as if they haven't pursued it with all the dignity and restraint of a rat up a drainpipe. Let's make this clear: unless one is born the heir to the throne of a reigning monarchy – and not always even then; who can name the heir apparent to the throne of Japan? – one has to work really hard at the fame thing. Having slogged to become so famous, it seems a bit rich – not to say simple-minded – to turn around twenty years later and whine about what a pile of crap it all is. Just go, then! – you're probably rich enough. Do what Sade Adu and Kate Bush did when they were at the height of their fame and genuinely grew tired of it – disappear!

The difference, I suppose, is that they weren't greedy and needy, unlike the moaning minnies who complain about fame while doing everything humanly possible to keep it at fever pitch. Hypocrite, heal thyself!

AMY WINEHOUSE KNOCKERS

Chas Newkey-Burden

There are few types of people more happy to throw stones from glass houses than pompous old men of rock, especially when these yesterday's men see someone younger than them having fun. You don't need to be a studious newspaper reader to have noticed that wonderful Amy Winehouse is having fun aplenty right now. As such she has become the target for disapproving outbursts from everyone from church leaders to politicians. Fair enough, I'd hardly expect the Archbishop of Canterbury or David Cameron to say, 'Go for it, girl! Get bang on it!' What has surprised me, though, has been the pitiful sight of rock's elder statesmen getting on their high horses about her. Plenty of men who have caned it for England have wagged their fingers at her. I'm sure Amy is absolutely beside herself that old rockers think she is a naughty girl. (Hope it doesn't drive her to drink or anything!)

Equally hypocritical are those fans who lined up to boo Amy during her winter tour of 2007. It's hardly a secret that her lifestyle is a bit on the chaotic and drunken side, so why did these people boo Amy when some of her performances turned out to be a bit on the chaotic and drunken side? Because they're hypocrites, of course!

GRAFFITI AND THE GUARDIANISTA

Chas Newkey-Burden

In times gone by, the Guardianistas could be seen at art galleries, staring at the exhibits, wondering how long they should spend looking at each piece of work and pretending they were enjoying the experience. During the 1990s, they got excited about Damien Hirst and his formaldehyde-bound animals. Sickening stuff, but not half as nauseating as the artistic idol of the modern hypocrite: Banksy.

Publications like the *Guardian* and the *Big Issue* treat Banksy with enormous reverence. The modern hypocrite believes that, by championing Banksy, they have moved out of the art gallery and onto the street. However, it must be easy to get all wet between the legs about graffiti when you don't live anywhere near the streets that are destroyed by vandalism. Few Guardianistas live in areas that are decimated by vandalism and therefore few of them are forced to pay increased council tax to have it cleaned up.

Due to his oh-so-edgy insistence that he remains anonymous, not a great deal is known about political-graffitist Banksy. However, enough is known to put him firmly in the category of the modern hypocrite. When he covered live animals in paint, did the animal-rights-supporting liberals who idolise him kick up a stink? No, because Banksy did it, and when he smears paint all over an animal it's different to when a vivisectionist does it.

When American It Girl Paris Hilton released her debut CD in 2006, Banksy replaced it in several shops with a CD featuring his own cover art and song titles that took a dig at Hilton, such as 'What Have I Done?' Well, Banksy, what she had done was set up a string of successful businesses, write a book and release an album all by the age of twenty-five. For someone whose supporters drool about how edgy he is, it was surprising when Banksy chose Hilton as a target. What was it about her that upset him so much?

Having a pop at a beautiful, happy-go-lucky blonde woman

will earn you brownie points among the modern hypocrites. But, when Banksy travelled to the Middle East to paint some images on the West Bank security wall, he earned their lifelong admiration. Supporters of the wall point out that its construction has coincided with a 90 per cent reduction in suicide bombings in Israel. Yes, it has caused hardships for some Palestinian people, but just for a moment imagine all those Israeli people who were not blown up as a result of it being built. Then imagine Banksy deciding that what the world needed now was for him to fly to the Middle East and do some silly drawings on it.

Describing the wall as 'the ultimate activity holiday destination for graffiti writers', he displayed a terrifying level of self-indulgence even by the standards of the Not In My Name brigade. However, any hopes that his nine drawings might make him a hero for the Palestinian people were dashed when a Palestinian approached him and the following exchange took place:

Palestinian: 'You've made the wall look beautiful.'
Banksy: 'Oh, thanks!'
Palestinian: 'We don't want the wall to look beautiful. We hate this wall. Go home.'

Oops! You can only imagine how stupid Banksy must have felt, but at least he could count on a hero's welcome when he got home. Not that he receives only praise: some have pointed out that his anti-capitalist stance is being increasingly compromised by his work for corporations and art galleries. I don't know much about art but I know what I don't like. And that is Banksy and his wanky followers.

POSH CONFESSIONALS VS COMMON KISS AND TELLS

Julie Burchill

Another month, another sob story; the embellished memories, from a once-respected publisher, of some poor ickle media-ocrity oofums – Tania Glyde, Tom Sykes, Sally Brampton, Paul Morley – who feels a bit mis and doesn't see any damn reason why the rest of us shouldn't suffer too.

And no, I don't mean the genuinely anguished memoirs of the type that followed *A Child Called It*; if people who've survived abuse of all kinds don't complain, all it does is make life easier for the kiddly-fiddlers, child-bashers and wife-beaters. And who but a repellent perve wants that?

No – good on the true survivors, let them sob all the way to the bank if it goes some way towards making up for the rotten hand they were dealt as children. The same goes for Jordan, with her trilogy of triumphant autobiogs, all before the age of thirty. Publishing them makes a different sort of sense: a) she's shameless and that's part of her charm, and b) she encourages working-class women to believe that they have exactly the same right to go for what they want, chavs or not, rather than trudge their joyless way through life cleaning up after people who do and suffering in silence, as proletarian broads have forever been expected to. And c) it makes total sense for the publishers as the whole lot of them sell like breast implants at a transvestites' convention.

Rather, I'm referring here to the endless stream of badly selling books regarding what I call Toytown Traumas; that is, sorrow which is either self-inflicted – drink, drugs, divorce – or which happens to so many of us as not to actually count as anything special – death of a loved one, loss of a job, divorce. Invariably they are written by journalists from the middle or upper-middle class, educated at some expense either privately or by the state; for some reason unfathomable to the non-hypocrites among us, middle-class and/or educated people who use their private lives for profit feel able to look down on working-class and/or uneducated people for doing the same, be they an incest survivor or a kiss-and-tell girl. But surely it's far 'worse' to blab if you're educated – because you have so many other options on how to turn a fast buck.

The fact is that this sort of bourgeois, bookish priss really wants to be admired – every bit as much as a *Big Brother* wannabe. But obvo, no one's ever going to admire them for any of the Three Big Bs that people tend to admire people for – brains, beauty and bravery. So – and you have to hand it to them for nerve, if for nothing else – they decide to market their very lack of these things.

Graham Greene saw a writer's childhood as his capital; the same can be said of a writer's troubles, whether random or self-inflicted. Until recently, partly because they were determined to demonstrate their skill and partly because they didn't want to have people pointing and laughing at them, writers used to take life's little pile-ups and make bad, banal or brilliant fiction out of them. These days – obviously every bit as affected by me-me-me, I-want-it-now short-termism as any Jade! – lots of writers can't be arsed to do all that creative stuff any more; rather, they bang out a 'memoir'.

Seven shades of mis – drink, drugs, eating disorders, dead parents, nasty parents, nice parents, growing up plain/pretty/dumb/smart; the steady drip-drip-drip of confessionals by the type of person who would, curiously, look down their snobby nose at Springer rednecks or strangers who show you their holiday snaps. And while most of us would agree that a pretty good working definition of a raging bore is someone who tells people they don't know their problems, for some reason these jokers seem to believe they're pretty damn fascinating. Above all, they seem to believe that they're in some way 'brave'. But what's so 'brave' about not being able to hold your drink and/or drugs and then whining about it! How can weakness ever be brave!

Your Jade Goodys and Chanelle Hayeses many not be heroes in that they didn't go into a burning building and pull out a puppy with their bare teeth, but they are certainly survivors of the type of childhoods that Dickens himself would reject as being too flamboyantly tragic. And yet we – well, you – of the chattering classes sneer at them as opportunists while lapping up the latest middle-class tale of self-inflicted misery. But your posh confessionals aren't 'survivors' in any real sense of the word – merely crybabies. Don't encourage these hypersensitive hypocrites, for goodness' sake; if you feel the need for that sort of indecent exposure, buy the Sunday tabloids and get it from some good unpretentious kiss-and-tell girl for a fraction of the price. Not to mention a fraction of the self-pity.

GREEN UNPLEASANT LAND

Cool Britannia; The Ex-Smoker; Mobiles and Emails; Chav-Haters; Hypocrisy towards the Homeless; The Hypocrisy of Nostalgia; The Bullying Hypocrite; A Right Royal Hypocrisy; Greens

COOL BRITANNIA
Julie Burchill

In all the decades I heard it, I was never once able to listen to the late lamented Radio 4 opening medley without seriously misting up. Wasn't 'What Shall We Do With The Drunken Sailor' a lovely touch? So typical of our unique self-deprecating sense of humour! Can we imagine the French, for instance, in the course of a daily national ident, referring to the national pixilation which leads to such atrocious rates of death from cirrhosis? 'Course not.

So you'll see from this that I am a rather trad sort of patriot. And, short of crypto-fascist movements co-opting the national flag as a camouflage for their own scummy and highly unBritish antics, I can't think of anything that gets my goat in this particular department more than a bunch of hypocritical middle-class media-ocrities attempting to find new ways in which to make patriotism – that squarest, sweetest of sentimentalities – trendy.

Cool Britannia was bad enough – and ended up by severely embarrassing every sucker who got within a mile of it. Then came the New Britishness, as touted by the *Sunday Times* in 2005, which was – deep breath! – 'passionate, complicated, intimate, thoughtful, self-reflective, a little bit wrong, a little bit funny, fond of a knees-up and emotionally literate'. Mmm, aren't we rather in Mom-and-apple-pie country here? – I mean, that could surely cover any European people from Moscow to Milan. And a whole bunch of Africans, Asians, Americans and whoever else, for all we know.

And then, in February 2008, *Grazia* magazine was pleased to inform us that BRITAIN ROCKS AGAIN: SUPERMODEL AGYNESS DEYN LEADS THE NEW COOL ARMY! Just as three years ago the *ST* twittered of the NB, 'We excel at collective moods and are very good at the details . . . we not only care about little things, we make them a priority' – as if that was something to be proud of! – now *Grazia* gushes, 'Britain is enjoying a brilliant new wave, a shining glitterball of creativity not experienced in the decade since Liam Gallagher and Patsy Kensit lolled on their Union Jack duvet on that iconic cover of *Vanity Fair* . . . the atmosphere feels future-focused, infused with androgyny, fluoro colours and edgy DIY glamour . . . although Boombox, London's super-cool dress-up club, has bowed out, its spirit lives on in the uncompromis-ing, exuberant styling beloved by the champions of Cool Britannia – the Britonistas.'

Yuck! – it's just so mimsy, so trendy-prissy, so namby-pamby, so Andy-Pandy, this new Britishness. I honestly think I'd prefer a red-blooded son or daughter of Albion to come out with a full-on anti-rant, as John Osborne did all those years ago – 'Damn You, England!' I think it was called. Surely that's a lot more interesting than being able to buy a Givenchy Limited Edition Union Jack Compact, £30, to commemorate Harrods' 'Truly British' event.

Say what you like about the old patriotism, but it was certainly democratic; the poor could be as flag-waving as the rich, the plain as the pretty, the old as the young, those who worked with their hands as much as those who skived with their brains. But looking at the photospreads accompanying such drivel, of 'the people at the grass roots who are effecting the rise of Britishness once more' to quote the *Sunday Times*, we see milliners, video directors, actors, sculptors, hacks, DJs and – snigger – handbag designers. Boy, I bet THEY'D have given the Luftwaffe a right old fright! All are, naturally, photogenic, self-promoting and under the age of forty. And this is what I find so revolting and hypocritical about Alternative Patriotism; this isn't about loving one's country at all, but about finding yet another way to be up oneself.

Cool Britannia totally excludes the poor, the old, the ugly; while purporting to be liberal and relaxed, it is guided by the twin principles of elitism and commerce. Which, I was brought up to believe, aren't that cool at all. Stick THAT up your funky fundaments, and leave patriotism to those who don't see it as yet another mirror to pull self-adoring faces in.

THE EX-SMOKER
Chas Newkey-Burden

The hypocrite – modern or otherwise – adores finger-wagging and one of the world's most enthusiastic finger-waggers is the former smoker. Despite the fact that these people have themselves polluted their own and other people's lungs for many years, they regard themselves as eminently equipped to have a go at those who still puff away.

This hypocrisy is deepened by the fact that few ex-smokers ever even bother to leave a decent break between giving up and turning on former smoking buddies. Maybe it's because they're in need of something to do with their hands but, straight away, they start wagging their fingers in smokers' faces.

'I'm right and you're wrong,' would be a fair summary of the ex-smokers' argument as they attempt to hound smokers at every opportunity. Interestingly, rarely have I heard someone who has never smoked get even minutely animated about the rights and wrongs of tobacco. It's just those hypocrites who used to smoke who are so quick to leap upon their high horses.

How they loved the smoking ban. To be frank, I hardly noticed the difference when it came in: few people had smoked in restaurants in recent times anyway. When they did, they were normally situated in clearly designated smoking areas that were easy to avoid if you didn't fancy breathing in their smoke. 'Think about kids in restaurants,' argued the anti-smoking lobby. So I did – and came to the conclusion that annoying kids are even more irritating in restaurants than any amount of smoke.

The anti-smoking brigade heralded the ban as the second coming and promised that once it was in place they would have no quarrel with smokers at all any more. 'As long as we can breathe in pubs and restaurants again, we'll be happy,' they said. However, within days of the ban coming into effect, they were back to their bitching and whining ways. 'I hate it because now all the smokers huddle outside the pub and so, whenever I walk past a pub, I get a face full of smoke.' I swear, these people won't be happy until all smokers are lined up against a wall and shot. And once that's done, they'll probably then start moaning about all the lost tax revenue!

Let's turn to the worst anti-smoking hypocrite of the lot: the ex-smoker who 'occasionally has one when I'm pissed'. I loathe these ghastly creatures. They bounce around all week, smugly blabbering on about how pleased they are to have given up smoking. They sneer at those they left behind in the land of smoking. However, the moment they get a bit pissed in the pub at the weekend, they are anxiously hunting down a smoker to cadge a fag from.

Great, isn't it? They get to feel all superior and smug about the fact they don't smoke. Yet when they're pissed they get to smoke. And here's the best bit: they don't even have to pay for the 'cheeky fag' that they cadge while pissed because it is the full-time smokers who hand it over.

At least your full-time smoker is honest about where they stand: they want to smoke and they will do so when stone-cold sober. The ex-smoker only does it when they're pissed, therefore treating it as a bad thing, something to get all regretful and morbid about the next morning. They're about as much fun as any other type of hypocrite: let's ban them from pubs and restaurants.

MOBILES AND EMAILS
Chas Newkey-Burden

We've all been there. On a crowded train when the enforced silence is punctuated by someone launching into a noisy conversation via their mobile phone. 'Hi, I'm on the train!' they roar, and the hearts of their fellow passengers sink at the prospect of being forced to listen to one half of an inane conversation. Particularly annoying is when such a chirpy chatterer bursts into exaggerated laughter at something the other person has said. Then there are those annoying ringtones, which are designed to suggest that the phone-owner has a personality, but which actually prove the exact opposite.

Still, I guess in a strange way we should be relieved when the 'I'm on the train' parade launch into their conversations. Often, these cheery chatterers are probably fulfilling some sort of exhibitionist tendency by talking so loudly on trains. Annoying as their conversations are, I'd much rather some-one satisfied their need for attention that way, rather than parading up and down the carriage showing off their private parts, or curling a steamy one on the middle of the aisle.

Another mobile phone annoyance is when you are dining or drinking with a friend, and he or she won't stop accepting calls or having text chats, as if you were not there. Obviously, this has never happened to me – I'm such electrifying company that my friends normally leave their mobiles at home when they come to meet me, honest! – but I would imagine that if it did, I'd be fairly horrified.

Fairly horrified, and fairly hypocritical, too. For my real annoyance would not be that someone is ringing or texting them, but that nobody was ringing or texting me. In the twenty-first century, one of the big fears for people is that nobody likes them. Perhaps an even bigger fear, though, is that it might be perceived that nobody likes them. Therefore, a friend receiving calls or texts while they are out with you is enough to stir up no end of insecurities.

I once had dinner with a guy who openly admitted that before any meet-up or date, he texts everyone in his mobile phone address book the message: 'Hi, how are you? Up to much tonight?' so he could receive a slew of texts throughout the evening. (His company was about as interesting as you would imagine from the above. I quickly made my excuses and left. I was amused when, three nights later, I got a text from him that read: 'Hi, how are you? Up to much tonight?')

At least he was honest, though. When any mobile phone user gets on their high-horse about someone else's use of their mobile, they really should take a look at themselves. They'd be gassing away into their own phones if anyone of their friends were to call. So perhaps the only people who are really entitled to take offence at mobile-use are those who do not own one themselves. The only two people I know in this category are my enchanting co-author, and her lovely hubbie, Dan. As non-mobile-owners, they would be quite entitled to throw things at me were I to use my phone in front of them. They never do, though. (Probably because I rarely get calls or texts whilst in their company. There must be bad reception in their part of Hove or something. Yeah that must be it. Can't be that nobody loves me!)

A related communications hypocrisy concerns email. There really are few more loathsome office creatures than the worker who returns from holiday, turns on his or her computer and spends the rest of the day sighing theatrically and saying: 'Oh, I've got so many emails to catch up on!' It's amazing how much of their day they can spend moaning about this. They stand by the water cooler, wiping their brow and noisily complaining about how many emails they have to catch up on. They pick up the phone and tell colleagues, contacts and friends how many emails they have to catch up on.

Then, finally, they get round to opening their email program. And send emails out telling everyone how many emails they have to catch up on. Their moaning about this fact is totally false – they're actually delighted about the situation because it reassures them that they're so important and liked! No matter that most of the said emails are photographs of cute kittens, or memos from the office manager about photocopier use policy!

Indeed, the whole concept of being busy has become riddled with nonsense and hypocrisy. Every time somebody starts an email: 'I'll keep this short, as I am very busy', they are contradicting themselves ridiculously. And as for all those Facebook status updates that read: 'X is up to his eyes in work', one cannot help but wonder how, if they are so busy, they find the time for Facebook. I try and avoid busy whenever I can, but when I have been under pressure, Facebook is the last thing I think of. But then busy equals cool in the eyes of many people nowadays.

People derive their sense of self-worth from many different sources: family, appearance, career, wealth, friends, humour and so on. They're all mostly valid in their own way. But those who can only get a sense of esteem by receiving phone calls on their mobile phones, or by getting lots of emails while on holiday are an absolute bore. Technology has got a lot to answer for.

CHAV-HATERS
Julie Burchill

No doubt about it – being non-racist is an extremely good thing. Sadly, over the past decade, an interesting number of those who passionately oppose racism in one breath have found no problem whatsoever in then firing vitriol and hatred at another group in the next – thus proving themselves to be utter hypocrites.

Yes, the white indigenous English working-class is the one group you can now insult with total impunity, the hot breath of the Commission for Racial Equality never coming anywhere near your soft Southern neck. Which makes the continuing trend for chav-baiting not just an act of consummate, cowardly bullying – 'Look – those people over there are the only ones without any protection – let's go and call them names!' – but also a new form of racism – what I would call 'social racism'. Hearing the baying packs of well-spoken radio DJs merrily dismissing poverty as 'sooo council', you could be mistaken for thinking that you are in some repellent parallel universe where all those soppy Christian ideas about all people being equal in the sight of God had never happened.

And they so rarely pick on the rich, even though the cretinous, braying behaviour of their youth is all around us, every bit as much as that of the sink estate hoodie. (And what's their excuse?) Maybe this could be because said DJs tend to be brown-nosing, forelock-tugging suck-ups who were obviously raised in their comfy lower-middle-class cribs to respect their wealthiers and betters. ROCK AND ROLL!

Every aspect of chav-hatred is riddled with hypocrisy. If a black person kisses their teeth, if a gay man comes out with a bitchy quip or an Irishman sings a daft song after drinking some green beer, they're all cheered to kingdom come for 'celebrating their culture'. Heck, they even all have annual holidays when they each, respectively, dance/prance/swagger through the streets to show us how proud they are of an accident of birth – sorry, their culture. (Ironically, the very word 'chav' may derive from the Romany word for boy, 'chavo'. And the Lord forefend that anyone shouldn't bow down in sheer molten awe before the Romany culture in all its glory unless they fancy a visit from the thought-police!)

However, should a person of English working-class origin dare to be anything but silently ashamed of their culture – and from music hall to Morrissey, from DH Lawrence to Ken Loach it must be said that in the twentieth century we produced at least as much as any other group, quite amazingly so considering our lack of formal education or stinking privilege – we're immediately taunted as 'chippy' and accused of 'going on and on' about our background. I can't think of one other group which is less encouraged to celebrate itself. And even as I say that, I can hear some seat-sniffing middle-class tosspot sniggering, 'Oh yeah – celebrating Paki-bashing, binge-drinking and turkey twizzler-eating!' But imagine the fuss if someone were to say that there was no point in Muslims celebrating their culture as it was all about daughter-murdering, hand-amputating and curry-eating!

Of course, another reason that it's considered 'safe' to hate-bait chavs is not only that the Commission for Racial Equality won't come after you, but neither will the chavs themselves – unlike other groups, who will fly into a murderous rage at the slightest, often unintentional, slight, and thus must be treated with kid gloves. That's because chavs, once you get past the fear-filled middle-class propaganda, are not half as violent as they're painted – in my experience they actually feel slightly sorry for their haters, who they see as castrated, desiccated, deracinated freaks incapable of having a laugh. And while domestic violence is shown by some surveys to be decreasing among the white working class, it is thought to be rising in the middle and upper classes.

Interestingly, considering how racist the white working-class is supposed to be, it's been a damn long time since a white working-class man killed his daughter for marrying or having a baby with a member of any ethnic minority – despite the great number of chav girls/council estate princesses/ Croydon face-lifted slags, according to your own particular prejudices, one sees pushing beautiful babies of colour in buggies. Whereas, oddly, one meets very few females from the higher, allegedly more enlightened classes who choose to miscegenate – funny, that.

In another instance of our inherent angels-with-dirty-faceism – rather than fascism – proletarian men are the only group who do considerably more childcare and housework than they did twenty years ago. For some unfathomable reason, middle-class professionals are actually doing less – mind you, all that pen-pushing and filth-downloading must make the poor dears absolutely exhausted. Who's got time to look after their own boring brats when they could be looking at exotic kiddy-porn on the company's time!

Nevertheless, despite our general sweetness of nature, everything we do seems to strike fear into a significant number of our better-educated brethren, who see malevolence therein and cast blame accordingly. In 1976, as a slip of a seventeen-year-old girl who had just started work at the *New Musical Express*, when I opened a can of Tizer – not even with my teeth, but simply by pulling the ring-pull! – I was beseeched by some middle-class no-mark: 'Hey man – stop flexing your roots!' In 2005, when I presented the excellent Sky One documentary *Chavs*, I was accused of being chippy, middle class and all sorts of silliness. When I pointed out that I was far too rich to be either chippy or middle class, it soon wiped the sneer off their sad-ass faces! Now the chav has become nothing less than an all-purpose whipping-boy who can be blamed as the source of all social ills. Thus, on 24 February 2008, in a *Sunday Times* magazine piece on why

Brits move to Australia, the journalist Paul Ham cited 'a brutally self-confident chav culture where good education and quality medical care are unavailable or unaffordable' as one of the reasons for the stampede. Honestly, blaming the unskilled working class for not providing good education and medical attention for the nation seems unreasonable enough. But claiming that one would flee to AUSTRALIA to ESCAPE from A BRUTALLY SELF CONFIDENT CHAV CUL-TURE? Lord love 'em, our aussie cousins – but isn't that a bit like going to a lap-dancing club to escape sexual stimulation?

Two days later on the letters page of *Heat* magazine, the nation's most reviled chavette Kerry Katona was used as the hook for similarly unhinged claims from the classy-sounding 'rob, Croydon' in which he accused Katona of being chavvy for having a bust-up with her mother-in-law and taking drugs; gosh, think of all the apparently posh people who've done both SO UNBEKNOWNST TO THEMSELVES ARE ACTUALLY SWITCHED BABIES! Elsewhere on the page 'anonymous desperate housewife of Sheffield' recounted how she had 'nearly wept' on discovering that Katona not only had named her baby Oscar (it was Max, actually) – as had ADH – but also had the same kitchen. 'Does this mean that I am a chav? Or does she have good taste?' the poor, painfully insecure lass implored readers.

It's a difficult one – but generally, I've noticed that calling someone a chav says far, far more about the abuser than it does the abused – who will more than likely be rather amused. And, amusingly, it pinpoints the area which the name-caller is most anxious about. Thus individuals who aren't getting much sex will hiss on about what slags chavs are, those who know that their job is one long skive (journalists are particularly culpable here) will bang on about how idle chavs are, and those who had long, expensive educations yet are now earning less before tax pa than Wayne Rooney spends on valet parking each year will bang on about how thick they are.

Everybody hates us, nobody likes us . . . but we're not going to be the ones eating worms. And it does make sense that we are discouraged from celebrating our culture and ourselves – unlike the other ethnic groups of poor economic origin who help make up good old mult-cult Britain – by being reminded ceaselessly what disgraceful, undeserving scum we are, because celebration is generally perilously close to having fun. And the modern hypocrite has always struggled with seeing his fellow countrymen do that – somehow, when they're foreign, it doesn't seem quite as bad, 'cause, like, they've got to do something to let off steam from living in nasty old Babylon.

Still, in the spirit of Christian charity, it's probably quite a strain living your life as a two-faced, duplicitous sneak, so chuckles must be at a premium in the household of our hypocrite chum. Little wonder, then, that they are so horrified when they see the white working-class having such a good time. And it must be doubly painful for these poor killjoys because not only are chavs probably the best at having fun, but we're exactly the people – according to outsiders – who should be too unhealthy, poor and prospect-free to enjoy ourselves.

What's 'worse', the chav lifestyle – live now, pay later, drink until you fall down unconscious in the street – seems to be making vast inroads into middle- and upper-class youth; the more attractive/bright/curious/bold of them, that is, not the sneering playa-haters with their tragic anti-chav websites. Rarely has a month gone by in the past five years when the *Daily Mail* has not run a two-page shock-horror spread about the rising inclination of girls from 'respectable' – i.e. middle-class – homes behaving like the very worst sort of binge-drinking ladettes and plastering their drunken antics proudly over the internet the next day. And as Amanda Platell pointed out in the *Mail* of 15 February 2008, above a photograph of an apparently drunk Prince William sitting at a table in Newquay's – Chav Central South-West! – Barracuda Club, littered with '14 empty alcopop bottles and countless discarded vodka shot glasses', it's not just the middle-class young who feel the call of the chav but even what Platell called the 'Binger-in-Chief, our future King, Prince William'. Impotently, and obviously unable to decide whether she was pro- or anti-monarchy, she stormed, 'What on earth was William doing in such a place? If he has no other function in life, it should be as a role model for the young.'

What indeed? Come on, Mands, it's pretty obvious what he's doing there – getting off his face, like the prince and the Englishman he is – but the 'why' is rather more interesting. It's because he looked at his role models – a good many royal males from the dawn of time till the present day – and saw a bunch of adulterous, deceitful, holier-than-thou hypocrites, who preach respectability for the masses and practise licentiousness themselves. The opposite of chav, in fact! It was hypocrisy which gave birth to the underhand evil committed against his late mother, whose life was probably smashed forever on the day that her husband told her that Princes of Wales 'always' had mistresses. Who can blame her son if he finds the bracing, straightforward vulgarity of chavdom preferable to the dreary, sneaky lies of respectability?

The chav-thinking, binge-drinking behaviour of the young British upper and middle classes terrifies the *Mail* because it so obviously isn't done out of desperation, as they might explain it away when done by working-class kids in an ex-manufacturing city or coal-mining ghost-town (killed off by the *Mail*'s heroine Mrs Thatcher, incidentally). It is done because it feels good. And then you stop, and you sober up, and you get on with your studies/work/career/being heir to the throne, whatever class you are. Your young body can take it, and take it it bloody will! But the simple maths of practical pleasure for some reason seem hard for tut-tutting hacks to grasp. Getting drunk in public, and not caring who sees? If girls from Girton and boys from Buckinghamshire can copy the hated chavs in this manner, who knows what class protocols they'll betray next? Maybe they'll lose their well-bred inclination to lead lives of quiet desperation, and cease to pursue 'good' jobs which end with them on their death-beds wondering what the point was – and where the fun was. They might even – Lawks-a-mussy! – be content to take the sort of low-paying, undemanding job that leaves them with time to live, Lord forbid, rather than spend every waking hour climbing the greasy pole to the air-conditioned misery of the top of the heap.

For, time and time again, those who score among the highest in job satisfaction surveys have what would generally be thought of as chav jobs; hairdressers, beauticians, plumbers, mechanics, builders and fitness instructors frequently feature among the happiest in their work, while resolutely non-chav architects, civil servants, bankers, IT specialists and – most consistently – lawyers appear to get the least kick out of their most well-paid jobs.

'So how come they can spend so much on clothes, with their crap jobs?' ask the haters, full of indignation and not a little envy as they drag their weary carcasses to yet another morning at their hated white-collar careers. Nothing changes;

in his great book *The Likes Of Us: A Biography of the White Working Class*, Michael Collins recalls how in the nineteenth century middle-class do-gooders berated the costermongers for spending 'too much' money on clothes for their children. And yes, the working class still spend 'shamelessly' – as they rightly should, for what class has worked harder for its money? And even if a minority of them scope out a few benefits now and then (funny how you never hear chav-haters objecting to the benefits bill for Eastern European migrants, which according to official Home Office figures hit a whopping £125 million this year – almost trebling in twelve months, even though even the most pro-immigration propagandist could not claim that generations of these people built and funded the Welfare State, as the indigenous working class obviously did), they certainly don't tend to be pimps and ponces. Unlike the other classes, who frequently make their moolah by waiting for their parents to die – ick! – or snapping up sweaty buy-to-lets in a bid to exploit the economic vulnerability of others. Perhaps it is their 'betters' who should be a tad more shamefaced with regard to their weird, status-obsessed spending habits, be it on five types of extortionately priced lettuce in a poxy salad, a king's ransom on a fortnight's living death in a mausoleum in Tuscany or blowing £200 a throw on having hot stones chucked at them, as many middle-class media madwomen are apt to do.

So to each his own . . . Chavs like to spend their leisure time drinking and spending, chav-haters like to spend their leisure time . . . hating chavs. Like, wow, what a worthwhile way to spend the day! And it is the increasing scale of fear and loathing towards the proletariat, conducted through the medium of modern technology, which makes this a truly modern hypocrisy. I'm a broad-minded broad, but I was amazed when my co-author told me that there were more than 500 groups on Facebook dedicated to attacking chavs, whose titles include ABOLISH ALL CHAVS SO THEY CANNOT BREED ANYMORE and DEATH TO THE CHAVS. These are no doubt offensive – imagine if they substituted MUSLIMS or indeed any other group for CHAVS! – but more than that, pitiable; it seems so very fitting that a website used mainly by bored office workers to while away yet another empty afternoon should be so full of hate for chavs. A more accurate title for such a group would surely be WHY ARE CHAVS HAVING SO MUCH FUN WHILE I HATE MY LIFE? AFTER ALL, I WENT TO A BETTER SCHOOL THAN THEM!

Elsewhere in the dark world of the internet, websites such as chavscum.co.uk demonstrate a very similar level of aggression and abuse to that which chav-haters accuse chavs of. I've noticed too that the odd little mole-men behind these sites often refuse to reveal their faces; you'd almost believe that they knew they were behaving in a cowardly, bullying, mob-handed, well, chavvy sort of way. Just as those who abuse chavs are hypocrites, so are chavs themselves strikingly lacking in that vice. 'If we weren't doing this, we'd be on the checkout at Tesco,' says the chav princess Cheryl Tweedy of the magnificent Girls Aloud. Can we imagine any bourgeois brat or posh prat of a pop star, any Lily Allen or James Blunt, saying anything half as self-aware about their amazing good luck, despite the huge amount of money spent on their educations? Naaah – for better or worse, right or wrong, pushing a beautiful black baby in a buggy with a fag hanging out their mouths or falling down drunk at their own teenage weddings, chavs are a people who surely anyone with an ounce of common humanity must love.

But by 2008, chav-hating had gained such momentum and was such common currency that it infected people who you never would have dreamed could be so snobbish and/or unself-aware – not just disappointed middle-class seat-sniffers killing time in boring white-collar jobs. A gay, Northern, working-class-born acquaintance of mine (albeit living in Brighton – Snob Central) would refer to a 'chavalanche' if a working-class family entered a restaurant where he was eating. A prostitute friend of mine, a mature and worldly woman of great sweetness and wit, whose beloved father had been an immigrant Irish labourer, complained bitterly of the indignity of having to share public transport with 'Croydon-facelift breeders'. When I went to a nail parlour with this lady, she advised me against having the 'squoval' (square-oval, and really very attractive to my untrained eyes) acrylic false nails I wanted as they were 'chavvy – what footballers' wives have'. When I chose them anyway, the young Vietnamese nail technician who applied them, and her Malaysian colleague who gave my sex-worker chum her tasteful, non-acrylic French manicure, reassured me vigorously that my choice was certainly NOT chavvy.

'No matter – I like chavvy,' I said casually. And one old white hooker and two young, chaste Oriental immigrant workers were united in their amazed, incredulous laughter. What a many-mawed, hyper-hypocritical beast is modern Britain's brotherhood of man: all peoples – bar one! – made one people by their shared loathing of the most powerless, silenced and demonised section of their society. O brave new world, that has such people in it!

And another thing . . .

'It's just a joke!' has always been the stock response from the chav-baiting rabble-rousers and ringleaders when accused of fermenting real social hatred against a powerless group of people. 'I'm an equal-opportunities insulter,' smirked an old Etonian hack with an extremely cushy life when I accused him of almost obsessively attacking chavs. This claim is never true; no race, no religion, no sexual orientation and certainly no other class is abused as routinely and revoltingly as the white working class, through the medium of the open-season get-out alibi of chav.

This climate of savagely specific abuse, as I've said, affected the most unlikely people. A survey in February 2008 by the Economic and Social Research Council, as reported by the *Evening Standard*, found that middle-class children whose parents made the 'risky' decision to send them to local 'demonised' comprehensive schools went on to do extremely well, with 15 per cent of them gaining places at Oxford or Cambridge.

However, despite the apparent lack of snootiness displayed by such parents in making this choice, their children rarely formed close friendships across class or ethnic boundaries. But even stranger than this, the middle-class parents who chose comprehensives for their children, 'mainly self-described "left-wingers" with degrees who worked in the public sector' as the *Standard* put it, shared the prejudices of other families who chose grammar or private schools. Many confessed to fearing the white working classes, whom they branded 'chavs' and 'white trash'. One London mother, named only as Vicky, admitted she felt 'sick' about sending her children to a comprehensive: 'You could say it's racism, it's classism, but with our local comprehensive it was fear . . . the first term I just felt sick, the whole time. I would like it to be the norm for people to go to their local school and not be scared the way I was scared.'

Many of these middle-class children, meanwhile, were reported by the *Daily Mail* – hardly a paper to accuse the bourgeoisie of being barbarians! – as regarding their 'chav', 'white trash' schoolmates with 'barely concealed disgust'.

Just a joke, for sure.

HYPOCRISY TOWARDS THE HOMELESS

Chas Newkey-Burden

The homeless have always been the target of abuse and vilification. However, in the olden days, your average tramp-bashing Tory was at least straightforward in their abuse. In the twenty-first century, the modern hypocrite is ultimately just as nasty towards the homeless, but in a far less honest way.

I've always thought that you can tell a lot about someone by their attitude to homeless people. There's quite a spectrum of depressing approaches: from those well-meaning types who delight in patronising them by using them to show how generous or caring they are, to those who as good as kick them in the teeth. All along the way, there are oodles of hypocrisy, too.

The first great hypocrisy towards the homeless comes from those who say, 'I don't mind giving them money as long as they do something entertaining as they ask for it. I don't like it when they sit there and just hold their hand out, begging.' Well, I doubt the homeless people themselves are finding the begging experience a whole lot of fun either, you wankers.

And as for 'doing something entertaining', what next? They can only have the price of a cup of tea if they pole dance for you? Why not just go the whole hog and start pimping them? Seriously, though, it's the equivalent of donating money to starving Africans but demanding that they 'do a little dance' for you in return, or dangling a tenner in front of a cancer victim and ordering her to tell you a joke.

A related bunch of hypocrites are those who give money to the homeless and then tell them what to spend it on. Just like the trend mentioned above, this one serves the multifunction of allowing the person to feel good about his or herself for helping while also giving them a definite feeling of power over another human being. However, if any of these people were to find a note from their boss in their pay packet saying, 'Don't go spending this on booze or sweets,' they'd, of course, be up in arms.

When people say, 'I'm worried they might spend it on booze or drugs,' I wonder what they expect someone whose life is so full of cruelty and pain to spend it on. A down payment for a mortgage? An Aga oven? It comes down to this: either give them some money or don't. But, for goodness sake, cut out the finger-wagging because what all homeless people need just as much as money is self-respect and, when you treat them like naughty children, you do untold damage.

A friend of mine witnessed an even more bizarre example of homelessness hypocrisy on a train. A homeless man entered the carriage and gave the standard pitch about needing money to get a room and how any help at all would be much appreciated. As he then made his way through the carriage, an earnest-looking woman stopped him and asked a lengthy series of concerned questions about him and how he became homeless.

Having finished her questions, she then turned away and carried on reading her paper, offering him no money at all. By this time, most of the passengers had alighted the train and the poor man's chances of getting any money were more or less reduced to nil. However, at least the earnest woman felt better about herself following her clever and concerned questions. The homeless, huh: as good as a self-help book but free of charge. How would we feel good about ourselves without them?

THE HYPOCRISY OF NOSTALGIA

Julie Burchill

I've said some excruciatingly cute, idiot savant-type things in my long, lurid and oh-so-quotable life, but one that especially sticks in my tiny mind is, 'If the past was so great, how come it's gone?!' And the more I see of the ever-creeping nostalgia industry, the less point I see in revising my opinion. What is truly creepy about modern nostalgia is that whereas in the past it was indulged in by the old – and you can easily understand people being dewy-eyed about the days when they could cut a rug rather than weave one, or when their hips weren't made out of Meccano – these days it's more likely to be the still-fit young and middle-aged who indulge, while their grandparents/parents are having a ball squeezing the equity out of the old homestead and blowing the kids' inheritance on sportswear and cruises.

From my forty-plus generation's obsession with Facebook and Friends Reunited to my thirty-five-year-old husband and his friends who come over all unnecessary at the sight of Bagpuss to the twenty-somethings who are prepared to sit through the 100 Best Whatever shows in their eye-watering entirety, when we're not wasting our own lives pining for the past, some of us are attempting to inflict this morbid neurosis on our children too, with retro lit-shit such as *The Dangerous Book For Boys* and *The Great Big Glorious Book For Girls*. Let's face it, British brats are self-pitying and pessimistic enough already, what with those ceaseless surveys telling them how hard their lush little lives are, without being encouraged to wallow in the entirely fictitious idea that things were better for kiddies in the past. Hmm . . . child chimney sweeps, little match girls and the gentle pleasures of the workhouse for orphans; what a shame we can't magic the ungrateful little darlings back to the good old days for a while. They'd soon start appreciating the alienation and fragmentation of horrid modern life after two weeks without their Nintendo!

It's got to the point where the nostalgic young – exhibiting all the arrogance and ignorance of their kind – are actually contradicting the progressive old. I recently heard a teenage misery-bucket on Radio 4 moaning on about how 'wholesome' life had been for da youf in the first part of the twentieth century. A charming old academic man who had actually been young during those years insisted to her that for the majority of people – the young, the old, the working class, women – life then had seriously sucked and that the modern world was much preferable.

But Miss Misery just wouldn't be told, illustrating another strange thing about nostalgia – and this would be where the hypocrisy element rears its ugly head – the idea that modern life is rubbish is touted with the most verve by the very people who have most benefited from progress. No less than two lesbian novelists, to my knowledge, have written in newspaper articles about their dislike of the 'modern world' – what on earth do they think their lives would have been like in the olde worlde, the question is begged?! For those who were not rich and/or powerful, life until very recently indeed was total rubbish – and it's highly unlikely that either of these ungrateful cows would have enjoyed the freedom to live their lives as lesbians, feminists or even novelists in the bygone age they appear to crave, humble as their origins are. No, they'd have been out of school at ten, up a chimney at twelve, illiterate all their lives and doomed to a living sexuality-denying death as a wife or a prostitute – if they were lucky. The one upside I can think of is that the world wouldn't have had to suffer their rubbish novels!

If a gay person pines for the 'good old days', does it make them a hypocrite, a fool or both? For it is only the modern world which has given gay people the right to follow their hearts, live their dreams and hold fast their freedom. The traditional world they increasingly extol, on the other hand, would have seen them living a lie and being forced by convention into joyless marriages – as wretched gay Muslims now are, in order to escape the laughably named 'honour killings' which plague their community.

It's not just the good-old-days-gays who have such a surreally selective memory. Open any glossy magazine and you'll find some dumb cow wittering on about how stressful it is having to vote once every four years, and why if only she was allowed to lick out toilet bowls wearing a Cath Kidston straitjacket she'd feel like a real woman for once. Well, I say to the lot of them: do us all a favour, you ignorant nostalgia freaks who should know enough about the dreadful oppression of your kind to appreciate the beauty of choice, but instead insist on bleating about what a 'tyranny' it is. Why not put your money where your moan is and move to one of the world's many Muslim dictatorships – there were more than fifty when I last counted – where you'll find old-fashioned values aplenty. And the real tyranny of limited choice – about what you wear, what you learn, how you worship, who you marry – to your drab little heart's content.

And leave the rest of us to look forward to the future with hope in our hearts and a giggle in our groins. Because you're history.

THE BULLYING HYPOCRITE

Chas Newkey-Burden

You don't have to be a bully to be a hypocrite, but my goodness it helps. The bullying hypocrite is very easy to identify: perennially dissatisfied with their life, to deal with that disappointment they seek out situations where they can find someone in a less powerful position and stamp all over them.

And where better to do this than in a restaurant? There's always something one can moan about if you really want to: the service is too slow, the service is too fast, the food is bland, the food is too spicy, the table is wonky, the glasses are warm and so on. I am not talking about polite feedback here; rather I am describing those who seemingly pitch up to a restaurant almost hoping to be disappointed so they can be rude to the waiter.

You can learn a great deal about someone from their attitude to waiters. Indeed, I'd go as far as saying that anyone who gets off on being rude to them is extremely unlikely to be getting off in any other areas of their life. In a survey of American CEOs, one of the few things they all agreed on was that people who are rude to waiters are bad news. Some of them interview potential employees in a restaurant to see how they treat waiters. Anybody who is polite to the CEO but rude to the waiters is immediately struck off the shortlist. Love it.

Then there are those at the other extreme of the scale: the people who feel ludicrously uncomfortable at the idea of being waited on, and therefore spend all their exchanges with the waiter apologising for even existing. Their underlying message is: I feel uncomfortable for your lowly position, so I am going to be all awkward and apologetic. It's bullying with the limpest of wrists.

While I'm sweeping the culinary board, perhaps the worst of the lot are those who say: 'You must never be rude to a waiter, or they'll spit in your food.' My, oh my, it truly comes to something in life when the only reason you can find to be pleasant to someone is because you fear they'll spit in your soup. What on earth happened to just being pleasant for pleasant's sake? And why do these people bother eating out at an establishment that they believe runs under some sort of saliva blackmail?

Therein lies the hypocrisy of all this: if eating out really leaves you feeling so consistently dissatisfied, then why not stay at home and eat there? Why not give your own kitchen a whirl? Nobody is forcing you through the doors of restaurants. So enjoy it or stay at home! But then I suppose hurling abuse at a saucepan in your kitchen would not be as fun as dishing it out to a real live human being, who cannot answer back.

Transport, too, is an area rich in opportunity for the bullying hypocrite. We are mostly all for the idea of people bringing in new rules to tackle traffic or parking ... until those rules are applied to us. Then, it becomes not just the work of evil fascism, but another great way to sound off at people who cannot answer back. Traffic wardens are sitting ducks for those who want to lash out verbally at someone. Likewise, when we cannot find a spot at a car park we're livid at the 'Full' sign, but if the staff try and remove any car that has outstayed its welcome, we react as if they have just lynched a small kitten.

It's much the same with public transport. When trains get delayed or cancelled, the bullying hypocrite finds the nearest representative of the train service and shouts and screams at them, regardless of the fact that it is not that person's fault. I wonder how any of these angry men – is it just me, or is it nearly always men who feel the need to let off steam in this way? – would feel if someone came to their workplace and shouted at them about something they had zero control over?

It's easy to scream at a ticket collector for a shabby train service, but I suspect that few of those who scream at them then go on to actually complain to the people really responsible for the bad service. And how many of us can say that when it comes to election time, we even consider candidates' or parties' policies on trains? Still, where is the fun in actually trying to change anything, when there is a defenceless ticket inspector to give the full hairdryer treatment to? And if the train delay means you're late home, you can always eat out.

A RIGHT ROYAL HYPOCRISY
Chas Newkey-Burden

It was *Private Eye* that captured the hypocrisy of the some of the public reaction to the death of Diana, Princess of Wales in August 1997. The front cover of the magazine featured a photograph of the crowd which swelled outside Buckingham Palace during the heady week which followed the Paris tragedy, with speech bubbles emanating from the crowd. 'The newspapers are terrible,' said one speech bubble. 'I know,' read another, 'I couldn't find one anywhere.'

There was a strong ring of truth to this cover. Many of those who spoke of newspaper editors having blood on their hands that week were the very paying punters who flooded the coffers of the *Sun*, *Mirror*, *Hello!* etc. every time they published a photograph of Diana. When it emerged that some paparazzi photographers had been chasing Diana prior to her death, I marvelled at the 'shock horror' reaction of some of these tabloid readers. Just how, I wondered, did they believe that the photographs they had so enjoyed gawking at had come to fruition? Through some sort of happy, chivalrous arrangement?

Diana's death has been widely credited with the ushering in of a new era in England, an era of touchy-feely emotiveness. Perhaps that's true, but another trend it sparked was that of royal hypocrisy. I am not writing here of any hypocrisy within the House of Windsor – when I wrote a bitchy profile of Prince William in the *Big Issue* magazine to coincide with his twenty-first birthday the fall-out was enough to put me off criticising that bunch for life – but rather our hypocrisy, as we stand either fawning or sneering at them.

The post-Diana era began with a scent of rebellion in the air. Previously loyal subjects began to question whether the royal family had any relevance any more. The Windsors' reaction to Diana's death was considered by some to be cold and uncaring. Here already was a colossal contradiction on the public's part. We know you do not care about her, the public seemed to be saying, but we want you to pretend you do. Tony Blair's line about 'the People's Princess' struck a chord with many. (And you reckon you first wrote that line, Alastair Campbell? I think you'll find my enchanting co-author coined it several years previously.)

However, it was in the years to come that the mood of the public did more turnabouts than Cristiano Ronaldo on a busy day. Having turned on the royals after Diana's death, the public was then won round by a Buckingham Palace PR campaign that cleverly positioned the Windsors as a modern, caring family. By the time Brian May was strumming his guitar on the roof of the Palace during that bizarre Jubilee concert, the mood had well and truly turned back in favour of the Windsors. No longer were we gathering angrily outside the Palace; instead we were lining up to offer 'Ma'am' our congratulations. And who could have imagined back in August 1997 that the marriage of Charles and Camilla in 2004 would be greeted with such joy?

Which is all well and good if that's what you're into. However, if you're going to go all pro-Royal on us, then at least have the good sense to know what you are getting into. It's a monarchy, it's hereditary: democratic it ain't. So it is hugely ironic that 'modern monarchists' believe they can both back the monarchy and have a say in how it's run. Many has been the time when I have heard someone say: 'I think they should skip a generation. Prince William should succeed the Queen.' Or some will say: 'When Charles becomes King, I don't think Camilla should be Queen.'

The desirability of these suggestions is not the question. What is at question is why people believe they can at once be pro-Royal and have a say in how it is run. That's the point of a monarchy: it's unelected and undemocratic. So either buy into it wholesale and accept they'll do what the hell they want, or oppose this undemocratic institution. Any other position is too riddled with contradictions to be worth having.

And another thing . . .

The panic over 'dangerous dogs' returned to our newspapers in early 2008. The heyday of this particular hysteria was during the 1980s, when Rottweilers and pit bull terriers were deemed the biggest threat to mankind. Photos of children's chewed faces were especially popular in the tabloid press. And – following a break to allow asylum-seekers to become public enemy number one – fido-fear is back again, and it is no less hypocritical than it was the first time round. Because every time a 'dangerous dog' is portrayed in the media, it is always belonging to a working-class family. It's as if dogs are perfectly tame animals whilst in the hands of the middle or upper classes, but put the sweet little darlings in a working-class environment and they become horrible, murderous and savage beasts. We know this is nonsense, though, because numerous poshos and even a member of the royal family have been convicted of dog-related offences down the years. And I think it's fairly likely that if foxes were given the choice of facing either a mob of hunting poshos and their pack of hounds, or any domestic dog, they would ecstatically choose the latter. The whole paranoia is barking mad.

GREENS
Julie Burchill

Throughout the joyful and rapid writing of this book, my brilliant collaborator has occasionally – and charmingly! –

reminded me that, alluring though the idea is, THIS BOOK MUSN'T JUST BE A LIST OF THINGS WE LOATHE! NO JULIE! IT CAN'T JUST BE ONE LONG RANT – OR EVEN LOTS OF LITTLE RANTS! WE'VE GOT TO KEEP OUR EYE ON THE BALL – IT'S ABOUT HYPOCRISY! JULIE – BEHAVE!

So imagine my delight, after ceaselessly checking my cruel intentions against the dictionary definition of this oh-so-slippery word, to arrive triumphantly at my final essay. To be presented with such a sumptuous smorgasbord of two-faced flimflammery as is incessantly displayed by the characters whose antics I am about to chronicle really is leaving the best till last and the somewhat smug phrase 'This baby's gonna write itself!' kept positively wrenching itself from my lips, no matter how I tried to resist. I speak, of course, of those people we popularly know as 'Green'.

Green . . . what a word to conjure with – so many meanings! According to the Online Dictionary of Slang, it can mean 'in agreement' – 'Are we green about this?' – or 'uncomfortable with sexual contact, for example afraid to kiss or touch private areas' – 'He's so damn green!' Answers.com supplies other definitions of the word, including 'money', 'lacking sophistication or worldly experience; naive – easily duped and deceived; gullible' and even 'having a sickly or unhealthy pallor indicative of nausea or jealousy'. And, of course, 'A supporter of a social and political movement that espouses global environmental protection, bio-regionalism, social responsibility and non-violence.'

It's this definition I'll be dealing with at length in this essay – hence all the hand-rubbing at the beginning. Because, in the constellation of modern hypocrisy, the Green shines a million times brighter than any of his half-hearted, two-faced comrades in duplicity. And it all comes so naturally! But, interestingly, all the other definitions I've listed reflect aspects of that one.

One: if one is NOT in agreement with Green views these days, one risks being thought of as an antisocial pariah far worse than a violent criminal – HE may have beaten up one person, but WE are repeatedly raping Mother Earth!

Two: Greens are supremely unsexy, their obsession with collecting rubbish and making-do the antithesis of reckless, romantic modernism – and their visceral, fascinated repulsion at the sexual behaviour and breeding capabilities of the masses sticks out a mile, even though at least two-thirds of them are filthy adulterers with four or more spawn.

Three: Green is the first socio-political movement in which EVERY SINGLE LEADER AND SPOKESPERSON is filthy rich – they make the Conservative Party look like the Jarrow marchers. Even the suffragettes – a pretty posh posse – could count working-class women among their star turns. But look at the Greens – not one chav champion in the whole stuck-up set-up that is chock-full of Etonians!

The new generation of Private Frazers – 'Doomed, doomed – we're all doomed!' – tend to be from massively wealthy families too, though their ancestors tend to be barons. It doesn't take Frasier Crane to work out that what these silver-spoon scions may be experiencing is a good old-fashioned bout of class guilt to make them turn on the cut-throat carpetbagging that made their families' fortunes. But whereas getting a dose of socialism would have led them to turn – quite rightly – on their own kind, the rich and powerful, the warped logic of ecology encourages them to turn on the poor and powerless. Hence the constant harping about how cheap food, cheap clothes and cheap travel are the enemies of the planet – so, presumably, prices should go up and the well-off won't notice a difference while the poor should starve, go barefoot and stay at home. Just like in the good old days, eh, chaps?

I've got to say – in what may be viewed as an uncharacteristically controversial point of view here – that I find something particularly weird about the idea of Jewish Greens. Even as a lifelong philo-Semite, surely I am not exaggerating in saying that the Jews are an exceptionally intelligent race – a quick glance at the number of Jewish Nobel Prize winners compared to the small number of them left in the world establishes this. Partly because of their great intelligence, they are overwhelmingly urban, modern and self-made – that is, the opposite of Posh, and thus the opposite of Green. So what happened with these particular spoon-fed noodle-brains? When one's family reaches a certain tax bracket, does one's rich side (dumb) just automatically take over from one's Jewish side (smart) and simply render one as intellectually unexceptional as any other beneficiary of inherited wealth? Whatever, it seems extraordinary for a Jew to be dewy-eyed about the allegedly good old days – which would have seen them barred from further education in this country, and would have found them chasing a skinny chicken around a shtetl back in the land of their fathers. That's when they weren't themselves being pursued to the death by Cossacks on horseback, of course.

And let's NEVER forget that the Nazis were the first Greens. They would've hated Tesco, and not just because it was started by a Jew. As Neil Davenport pointed out on the online magazine *Spiked*:

> Back in the 1930s, one political party did rise to power promising to rein in the 'excesses' of chain stores. The

Nazi Party passed The Protection of Individual Trade Act in May 1933. From then on, chain stores were forbidden to expand or open new branches. They were also forbidden from offering a discount of more than three per cent on prices. Essentially, small shopkeepers in Germany, together with their middle-class supporters, wanted the state to claw back some of the prestige and status lost through the expansion of industrial society. It's not too fanciful to suggest that the Nazi Party wouldn't have looked favourably on Tesco, either.

Four: lacking worldly experience. I'll say! Largely because – see 'Three' – their wealth is generally inherited.

Five: that sickly pallor of nausea and jealousy that glints through despite the extortionately priced organic diet – it's contempt for humankind, pure and simple. And here's more hypocrisy: it's usually, in my experience, exhibited by people who really have very little right – intellectually or morally – to look down on anyone.

Because, more than anything, Greens are hypocrites. This is beyond debate. The only question is – do they actually know that they are hypocrites, or are they so damn dumb that they have no idea? And which is worse? Hypocrisy is historically viewed as a somewhat knowing intellectual position ('The tribute that vice pays to virtue' – as if hypocrisy itself was not also a vice, which muddies the waters somewhat) but surely it's possible to be a dumb hypocrite – and, if you are, do you actually count as one or are you just a cretin from whom it would be almost unfair to expect logic?

But no matter how many Greens can dance on the head of a pin, the point is that they remain the absolute yardstick of cutting-edge modern hypocrisy. It's just like the glorious

Jeremy Paxman said of the BBC when he claimed that the Corporation's environment correspondents 'travel the globe to tell the audience of the dangers of climate change, while leaving a vapour trail which will make the problem even worse', just after thirty-seven BBC staff were sent to cover an economic summit at a Swiss ski resort.

Despite the amount of human anguish in the world, nothing appeals to the rich the way Greenery does. This is because Greenery actually reinforces the prejudices of the elite about the masses: that they are intrinsically 'spoiling' everything simply by doing things – breeding, travelling – that the rich seem to believe should be reserved exclusively for VIPs. It's yet another snobby variation on the way that 'the great and the good' (who are usually also the greedy and the goody-goody) are absolutely fine with things like divorce and abortion when only they have access to them. Then the masses get their mitts on these choices, and it's Fall-of-Rome time!

It is no longer acceptable for the rich to boss around the poor simply because of their respective economic status – but, oh joy, it turns out that you can lecture and scold them in the name of the planet and *they* look like the villains of the piece if they argue back or refuse to obey you. In the winter of 2007, it emerged that the top three recycling boroughs were well-off Bexley, Bromley and Sutton, and the worst three recycling boroughs were Tower Hamlets, Lewisham and the charming-ly named East London Waste – nasty, wasteful poor people! The Tories can no longer trust their poshness to ensure that the un-posh let them run the country, so they must play the caring card and fight Labour on their ground. But rather than do the obvious things that would really indicate that they care about people, such as agreeing with Labour that there should be a minimum wage, they have come over all Green, and thus feel free to boss the poor once more with impunity.

When politicians try to use Greenery to appeal to women voters, they are truly insulting. Green policies, if pursued with any real vigour, would be disastrous for women, and though they may pay lip service to its caring, sharing sentiments, they instinctively know what awaits them if they give up the triumphs of modernity. No tampons, no disposable nappies, no mod cons – and no time to do anything that actually smacks of FUN! as we waddle between recycling boxes, compost heap and scrubbing board.

Greenery isn't just preached by hypocrites, it makes hypocrites of the people it seeks to corral – that's why 90 per cent of Londoners say they recycle paper and glass, while only 20 per cent of either gets recycled. That's why newspapers reported that Marks & Spencer – which started out in 1884 with typical Jewish-immigrant honesty and initiative when a refugee from Poland called Michael Marks started up a stall in a Leeds open market selling haberdashery, toys and sheet-music under the legend DON'T ASK THE PRICE – IT'S A PENNY – said of their signing for a six-figure sum the lovely size eight, nineteen-year-old model Lily Cole as the face of 2008 that it was as much to do with her environmental credentials as with the way she looks; she is patron of the Trees For Cities foundation and wrote the foreword to *Green Is The New Black*, a book about 'ethical shopping'.

Green is the white man's Islam: really agreeable for the rich, who have servants to do everything boring for them, and really super-sucky for everyone else, especially women. Yet rich women who espouse Green causes can be the biggest hypocrites of all, smug in the knowledge that, if they tick the Earth Mother box with enough conviction, they can then play

Marie Antoinette to their heart's content. Can it be that these clowns' contempt for the public is so deep-seated that they really believe their hideous hypocrisy will go undetected no matter how little they attempt to conceal it? How astounding that they feel it appropriate to queen it over the rest of us.

Rich people who espouse Green causes yet go on accumulating wealth are hypocrites, as are all Green women who enjoy the benefits of modern life. Like Islam, Greenery is terrified of modernity because it knows in its heart of hearts that it is no match for it.

Yep, while that bitch Mother Nature is doing everything in her power to screw up a gal's fabulous life, it is modernity that pushes us forward and watches our backs – the driving force behind the increasing freedom and progress of femalekind. The ideal Green gal, like the dream Muslim Mrs, is barefoot and pregnant – and after the Gaia-groupies have got rid of all those evil, energy-squandering, time-saving devices, we'll all be far too busy a-cookin' and a-cleanin' in true Stepford Wife-style to get any highfalutin ideas about careers, Open University courses or extra-curricular cock.

There's a saying – 'Life's a bitch and then you die'. Contrary to the best efforts of the Green Cow Contingent to convince us otherwise, life for the vast majority of women in pre-industrial society – the Green Arcadia – was a vale of tears, blood and excrement. And then you died in childbirth! As for the Green female vote that politicians are courting – in my book, any woman who wishes to return to this fetid state of affairs should have their vote removed forthwith. Because surely the poor things are criminally insane.

Us broads are fragrant creatures – and as we contemplate the likely end of weekly rubbish collections and the vermin-fest that seems likely to follow, we already face a far smellier future than we envisaged. I've spoken of how the rich invariably preach about becoming Green while continuing to accumulate wealth and enjoy lavish lifestyles, but almost as vile and hypocritical are the antics of bureaucrats, local and national, when they attempt to inflict Greenery on the wretched populace. Though chivvying-prefect bossy rather than lord-of-the-manor snooty, they equally deserve a punch up the bracket and compost shoved where the sun don't shine for daring to presume that they know better than us.

Consider my own home town, of Brighton and Hove, a place where Green bullshit reigns supreme beside the shining sea. Not a new day seems to dawn without a new ecological initiative being thrust on the unfortunate citizens of this burg. This can be anything from the council voting to ban plastic bags – and we can use all the dog muck that their owners leave behind once these useful receptacles are no more to fertilise our yummy organic veg, no doubt! – to the local Green party shamelessly bum-sucking up to thousands of Poles who work here for their vote in a winter 2007 local by-election – ZAG-LOSUJNA PARTIE ZIELONYCH!

Regrettably, the would-be flattering remarks of the Green candidate, one Jason Kitcat – 'We very much welcome their work ethic . . . Poles have a deep-seated appreciation of nature and connection with the seasons. Their dedication to traditional skills, seasonal foods and love of the countryside connects them with the core values of the Green Party' – came across a bit blood-and-soil, bringing back bitter memories of how Poland's anti-Semitism and rabid nationalism were historically, in Europe, second only to that of the Nazis. It also gave the unfortunate impression that Mr Kitcat was doing an oh-so-familiar bit of chav/Brit bashing by implying that our own people were workshy and unskilled – not to mention raising the obvious question of how a party that bangs on ceaselessly about the importance of roots, local autonomy and the evils of globalisation can think it either appropriate or desirable for foreign citizens and guest workers to vote in an election which will determine the immediate future of a small part of Sussex. You're not even meant to eat an APPLE from outside the county if you're a Green – yet somehow a vote is a moveable feast!

Get off the train, queue for a taxi and you're staring at a huge billboard for something called zerofiftyone.com – 'the environmentally friendly advertising agency'. (Advertising types, so notorious for their sky-high BQ – Bullshit Quotient – and their feelings of overweening, albeit totally groundless, superiority, have embraced Greenery – LONG LIVE THE CAR. LONG LIVE CITRÖEN. LONG LIVE THE PLANET – with all the enthusiasm of organic pigs in muck, for obvious reasons.) Just across from this is the 'brighton eco centre' – no capital letters in either case, you FASCIST! And here we get a real sense of the filthy, mealy-mouthed Green hypocrisy to be found in this beautiful, once honestly sleazy, town.

Just a few years back the stench from uncollected rubbish rose over B&H like a particularly irresistible metaphor; the allegedly Labour council had for some reason seen fit to privatise rubbish collection, despite the disastrous results this has been seen to have on standards of hygiene from high street to hospital. The French company which won the contract had a real flair for royally fucking things up, managing to annoy B&H's notoriously noble and good-natured binmen with sackings and reschedulings to the point where they went on strike, while also making losses of around £250,000 a week. The garbage lay stinking in the streets for weeks and, when the binmen offered to work for nothing and clear the trash from the streets on a voluntary basis, the trash in the council offices said no, lest it upset the French franchise holders.

But we shouldn't have been looking at the rubbish festering in the gutter, should we? No, we should have had our eyes fixed on the stars! Or rather on the council's latest gimmick – the search for nine residents of B&H who wanted to 'change their lives over nine weeks – whether it's by getting fit or using the car less, saving energy or recycling more'. Gushed council leader Ken Bodfish, 'In true TV makeover fashion, we have drafted in a team of experts from personal trainers to organic gardeners, to guide the volunteers through the highs and lows of their own personal challenges.' The lucky nine were then given camcorders with which to make video diaries of their own personal 'journeys'; the purpose of the whole spectacle was to get across the message of 'Sustainability – ensuring a better quality of life for everyone, now and for generations to come'. As opposed, one presumes, to being wiped out by a twenty-first-century plague spread by super rats grown robust on weeks' worth of uncollected garbage.

Spending untold pounds of public money on Green gimmicks while all around the infrastructure of a civilised society crumbled – all hemp cape and no knickers – may have started here but, by 2007, the madness had spread nationwide. More than 3,500 council staff have now been hired throughout Britain, at a cost of around £100 million of our own money, basically to scold us, while at the same time councils implement savage cuts on such unimportant fripperies as social services, libraries, meals on wheels and – ta-dah! – free weekly rubbish collections. (Started in 1875 by Disraeli's Conservative government, fact fans!) While more than half the soldiers serving this country now buy their own kit because the standard issue is inadequate, and old people who have served their country in war and peace die in their own excrement on hospital trolleys, their country prefers to spend its – or our, rather – money on teams to go into schools and natter to brats about 'environmental issues' (that'll make the self-righteous little skivers even more unbearable than ever!) and thousands of pounds advertising for a 'carbon reductions adviser' to nag at businesses and charities about how to reduce energy consumption. No wonder the council-tax bill has almost doubled in the past ten years and there seems to be so little to show for it in terms of real welfare for the poor, old and wretched among us. But hey, just let those worry-warts at Help the Aged warn that they are 'deeply worried' about councils slashing the number of elderly people eligible for carers to help them at home – why don't the old fossils just take a day trip to London and visit the £200,000 Green Living Centre recently opened by Islington council, designed as 'a springboard to inspire individuals to take positive action towards a greener lifestyle'? Check out that ceiling made of 1,200 empty water bottles! – that'll send the crumblies home full of faith in the future, surely.

It's all just so inefficient, ironically, for a creed which prides itself on being a shipshape, make-and-mend, short sharp slap in the face of wanton wastefulness. And this lends yet another layer of hypocrisy to Green; the practice as well as the theory is rotten. In Brighton and Hove, where the council threatened in 2006 to fine people who threw away 'too much' rubbish – that is, left extra bin bags next to wheelie bins – there was a three-month waiting list for recycling boxes in 2007. Up the road in London, it transpired in October 2007, 75 tonnes of organic waste left by residents to be collected for composting had been dumped in a landfill by Harrow council – because 'too many' people were recycling. And so it goes, all across what is slowly but surely becoming this Green, unpleasant land.

For the promise of a better tomorrow for the wealthiest, most powerful and idlest in our world, Green is spoiling the lives of the poorest, weakest and most hard-working today. Far from being a revolution, Greenery is a savage defence of privilege and tradition. That those who espouse it rarely even bother to pretend to disguise their double standards demonstrates the extent of the breathtaking contempt they have for the 'masses' – that is, the people who do the work and pay the taxes which keep the very society that they live off, be they pop-star ponce or council bean counter.

This piece is so long compared to the others in this book, and took me so long to write, because of the sheer volume of choice I was presented with when I set out, three weeks ago, to write this essay on Green hypocrisy. Go back to the start, and marvel at my childish glee at the prospect of fairly romping through it: 'It'll write itself!' I believe I chortled. But as it turned out it was more like painting the Forth Bridge – every time I thought I was about to finish, I'd open a newspaper and find half a dozen more examples.

So here's where I draw the line, lest this essay become a book in itself. To sum up, this country at the start of the twenty-first century isn't Cambodia in Year Zero, and I don't believe that the inherited rich should be barred from public life and/or politics. But when they make up all of the leadership of a political movement, we should be sceptical – very sceptical.

The rich are Friends of the Earth because it's been a damn good friend to them – and they want more than anything to hold on to what they have and pass it on to their spawn. Not the starving kiddies of the Third World – theirs. They hear that the world might not be in such good nick in a few years' time, and their first instinct is to protect what they feel is theirs from the swarming masses. This makes them selfish. But the fact that Greens seem to think their own emissions don't stink – or count, as they fly around the world making speeches telling the masses not to fly around the world – is what makes them hypocrites of the most flagrant and shameless kind. Nothing illustrated this better or more sickeningly than the 2007 UN Climate Change Conference on the beautiful island of Bali, which ran from 3–14 December, involved 15,000 politicians, civil servants, campaigners and television crews being flown in – and generated the equivalent of 100,000 tonnes of extra CO_2. Which, as the *Sunday Times* reported, is similar to the entire annual emissions of the African state of Chad. Chris Goodall, the carbon emissions expert who did the calculations for the *Sunday Times*, said, 'One wonders how many people would have gone if the conference had been held in a wet October in Pittsburgh.'

Greens have no interest whatsoever in making things better for other people – just for the planet, which they see as a possession to be protected from other people. It is interesting that no Green I can think of has a background in any other sort of political movement, be it working for the rights of people to join trades unions or the rights of people not to be tortured for their beliefs.

Greens don't hear the screams of people, it seems – they're deafened by the wailing of plants and the cries of the planet. A vile alliance of the filthy rich and the mind-bogglingly bossy is now practising hypocrisy on a scale previously undreamed of – and, in the process, under the guise of making life better for future generations, it is making life worse for the poor, weak and wretched of today. As someone once said of anti-welfare anti-abortionists, 'They believe life begins at conception and ends at birth.'

I had planned to end this monster essay with a burst of my trademark verbal pyrotechnics, but then I read something which made me mute with fury. Suddenly, showing off seemed in the worst possible taste – it is, after all, showing off about being Green which led this thing to happen in the first place. In the autumn of 2007 the *Sunday Times* carried a story, by a reporter called Dean Nelson, writing from Delhi, which started thus:

'Pumping furiously on a foot treadle in the afternoon heat, six-year-old Sarju Ram is irrigating her impoverished family's field, improving the crop and – without knowing it – helping environmentally sensitive holiday-makers assuage their guilt over long-haul flights to dream destinations.'

Sarju's family is a 'beneficiary' of a group that aims to allow Westerners to offset their carbon dioxide emissions by funding 'sustainable energy projects'. The 'benefit' Sarju's family receives is that they give up their labour-saving diesel pumps and instead put their kids to work on the foot pumps. Reading about little Sarju and her siblings slogging in the sun in order that rich Westerners may holiday without guilt made me wonder if there is any level to which the Greens will not stoop in their hateful, hypocritical quest.

Not that it's just kids who are put to work on the foot treadles. As a spokesman for the company said approvingly, entire poor families are 'mucking in'. And all so rich Westerners can sleep easy on their private jets! When confronted about the hypocrisy and sheer wickedness of a scheme that puts impoverished little children, barely out of their nappies, into the most gruelling of work, the spokesman said, 'The phrase "child labour" is emotive.' It sure is, dude!

In Tudor times, the royal court would employ 'whipping boys'. Any time the heir to the throne misbehaved, these unfortunate souls were ordered to bend over and take a caning on behalf of the naughty heir, who himself went unpunished. A favourite phrase of the modern hypocrite is 'in these enlightened times'. Well, in these enlightened times we have impoverished Indian children slaving in the heat of the sun in order that an heir to the throne and the rest of us Brits can enjoy our lifestyles without guilt. They are nothing short of whipping boys for the twenty-first century, not just for the heir to the throne, but for any of us who care to get involved in the hypocrisy-ridden Green movement. 'They suffer, so we don't have to,' would be an apt slogan for this venture.

Not in my name.

APPENDIX

Hypocrites' Five Fave Footballers; The Hypocrites' Party Manifesto; Hypocrites' Holidays; Top Five Anti-Hypocrites; The Hypocrites' Ultimate Weekend

HYPOCRITES' FIVE FAVE FOOTBALLERS

You don't need to be a hypocrite to be loved by hypocrites, as these football folk prove!

1. Paul Gascoigne

It's typical of football's strange sense of priority that, during his chequered career, the crime that Gascoigne has attracted most abuse for was eating a doner kebab on the eve of the 1998 World Cup. Never mind that he admitted beating his ex-wife Sheryl, the fact that he ate a kebab is his real offence in the eyes of football folk. Cheers!

2. George Best

Oh, look: another football genius and another wife-beater! Best was a wife-beater and cheat who once quipped, 'I think we all like to give the wife a smack.' But, hey, let's not allow that to break up the party, nay, the orgy of Best-worship that continues to this day. How Michael Parkinson must have missed having the chance to invite Best on for yet another fawning interview, leading to the horribly inevitable, 'Tell us that story about Miss World and the room-service man. Go on! Just once more!'

3. Graeme Le Saux

The *Guardian*-reading Le Saux is an icon for the modern football fan. The wave of new fans who became attracted to the game in the early 1990s soon showed themselves for the hypocrites they were. Having flocked to a sport that was traditionally working class, they were quick to idolise those they called 'intelligent footballers', which was just their polite way of saying middle-class footballers. Le Saux, with his *Guardian* fixation and delicate manner, was a perfect example of this. Guys and gals, if it's middle-class sportsmen you want, I believe there are plenty in rugby and tennis. So gather up your copies of *Observer Sports Monthly* and your *Fever Pitch* first editions and sling your hook.

4. Jack Charlton

It might seem strange that The Pogues, a band with less than a 50 per cent Irish line up, were chosen to sing the official song for the Irish football side prior to the 1994 World Cup Finals. But it's actually very apt, because Jack Charlton's team took full advantage of FIFA's lax rules governing nationality and filled the Ireland squad with players who were about as Irish as Diego Maradona. As the national anthems before one match were played, so the story goes, one of Charlton's 'Irish' players turned to his teammate and said, 'This one goes on a bit, doesn't it?' only for his teammate to reply, 'Shut up! This is our one!' Nevertheless, the proud-to-be-Irish, Republican-ditty-singing supporters of the national team hero-worshipped Charlton, despite the fact that he Anglicised their team.

5. Testimonial players

'He's been a great servant to the Club,' is the customary plaudit for any player who is having their testimonial game. Hmmm, not sure many servants get paid £100,000 per week! And why should multi-millionaires have a testimonial, anyway? Fair play to those, like Dennis Bergkamp and Niall Quinn, who donated their testimonial dosh to charity. As for the rest, if they want to be called servants, isn't it time they were paid accordingly?

THE HYPOCRITES' PARTY MANIFESTO

Described as everything from 'a glorious mass of contradictions' to 'the most hypocritical suicide note in history', the election manifesto of The Hypocrites' Party is a key piece of political literature. Here we reprint its highlights.

EDUCATION

We oppose private education, apart from when it comes to our own children.

FOREIGN POLICY

We believe that it is not our place to criticise any foreign country or culture. Except Israel and America, who must be slammed at every opportunity. Our policy towards terrorism is thoroughly intellectual and mindful of the complexities of the myriad issues involved. In short, it can be summed up thus: if anyone bombs us, give them what they want.

CRIME
We would reduce the time that police are allowed to hold terror suspects from twenty-one days to twenty-one seconds. If they cannot build a case that quickly, then they shouldn't be in the job.

THE ENVIRONMENT
We plan an extensive, nationwide tour to tell everyone how bloody naughty they are when it comes to the environment. You should see the coaches we've booked – hyyyuge!

CIVIL LIBERTIES
The rights of women and gay men are important and inalienable – unless the expression of them is considered Islamophobic. In which case – burn the bastards and bitches! Cartoons must be banned from all newspapers.

ECONOMY
We pledge to embark on a colossal spree of public spending and will simultaneously cut all taxation. It'll work, just you wait and see.

HEALTH
As ex-smokers, we passionately oppose smoking and cannot work out why anyone would ever do it. However, we propose to bravely put our opposition to one side and take the tax revenue that smokers raise.

TRANSPORT
We cycle. Ergo, we are nice people. And you're probably not.

ARTS AND CULTURE
Arts: Banksy to be allowed to paint anywhere, apart from where we live.
Culture: Oh, reality television is so common, isn't it? Did you see *The X Factor* last night? Us too! Wasn't it terrible?
Sport: We've supported Arsenal for, like, three years!

HYPOCRITES' HOLIDAYS

Hooray, hooray, it's a holi-holi-day! Everyone loves a few weeks off in new surroundings and hypocrites are no different! Always remember, however, that the hypocrite is never a tourist but always a traveller. Got it? Good. Pack your bags and prepare to visit the destinations of double standards!

1. South America
With all those jungles, this region is the place to go for the Green hypocrite. You can even plant a tree in your name to help the environment (because it is, after all, all about you). And thanks to fuel-guzzling air travel, it's all only a matter of hours away. Remember to take your Sting CD to listen to on the flight!

2. Dubai
No self-respecting hypocrite would want to go to nasty, soulless capitalist America on holiday. So hurry up and book yourself a fortnight in stunning Dubai, which brings you all the joys of America but allows you the street cred of having travelled to an Arab state. There are plenty of skyscraper hotels to stay in, shopping opportunities galore and why not

take in a play at the Dubai World Trade Centre? That'll show Bush!

3. Majorca

As we know, standards of parenting and education have slipped in Britain. To avoid the summer influx of ill-educated, lawless British hoodies, make sure you visit during term time and not school holidays. It's cheaper that way, too. Granted, that'll mean you have to take your kids out of school for two weeks but they'll thank you for it later in life.

4. Africa

My goodness, you're right on if you go to Africa. Remember to haggle with the locals during every financial transaction. You're there to enjoy yourself and, after all, there's no greater feeling in the world than haggling a poor African man out of three pounds!

5. Arab States

You love their culture and believe that the sheer authenticity of it makes Western values seem so corrupt and futile in comparison. And, if you ask around in the right places, you will be able to find those underground bars that illicitly serve alcohol. Cheers!

6. India

The Taj Mahal, the deserts, the mountainous Himalayan regions and the garden city of Bangalore. It's lovely. Those bloody beggars almost ruined it, though.

7. France

The joy of France is that the owners of every bar and restaurant you visit will happily join in with you in a good old bitching session about how jumped up, colonial and dumb America is. The best part is, pretty much everyone in France speaks English so you don't even have to learn the lingo to join in!

8. Jamaica
They jail people for being gay here, don't they? Who cares – there are real black people on the beach singing reggae songs!

9. Ireland
I've stayed in hotels all over the world with my boyfriend. Our same-sex status has never even raised an eyebrow anywhere, including small guesthouses in the southwest of England, a chain hotel in the Midwest of America and even a hotel overlooking the Old City of Jerusalem in Israel. We even stayed in Tunbridge Wells without trouble, for goodness sake! However, there is one place where we're always guaranteed hassle – Ireland. The only reason we've ever gone there was so I could run the marathon, but completing the 26.2 miles proved easier than checking into a hotel as a gay couple in the supposed 'land of a thousand welcomes'. Naturally, the modern hypocrite overlooks all this bigotry and also ignores the unpleasant attitudes to women and abortion in the Emerald Isle. Why let all that ruin a good holiday? Slainte!

10. Warsaw
They say that this city is 'the new Prague'. Anti-Semitism and homophobia thrive in this city – in many parts of eastern Europe you can still buy icons of rabbis with blood on their mouths from eating Christian children. Yet the modern hypocrite will still flock there for 'the marvellous culture' (read: cheap booze). Not that their love of travelling to

Poland will prevent them from moaning about Poles coming to the UK.

TOP FIVE ANTI-HYPOCRITES

1. Simon Cowell
Nobody could accuse pop's Mr Nasty of being publicity-shy or financially temperate, but his pursuit of fame and fortune has always been beautifully transparent and consistent. Unlike those who claim to be in the business for the love of the craft, yet are more bothered about pound notes than musical ones, he happily admits he can go for weeks without listening to music for pleasure. He's also always stuck true to his belief that once you seek out the spotlight, you cannot moan about 'the downside of fame'.

2. Joe Strummer
Back in the punk days, The Clash fetishised terrorism in songs like 'Tommy Gun' and in their clothing and imagery. However, after the 9/11 attacks, Joe held his hands up and told his biographer Chris Salewicz: 'We have to go and get these people who did this. We sat back and let the Nazis do what they did. We can't make the same mistake here.' Woah, Joe: rock the casbah! Rest his soul.

3. John Pantsil
The 2006 World Cup was – glorious WAG Melanie Slade aside – a bit of a bore. Until, as Ghana played the Czech Republic, Ghana defender John Pantsil celebrated both his team's goals by whipping out an Israeli flag and waving it with joy. He played for Israeli club Hapoel Tel Aviv and wanted to

say thanks to the great nation that had made him so happy and to the Israeli fans who had travelled to Germany (of all places) to support him. As modern hypocrites around the world erupted with fury at Pantsil's gesture, he smiled: 'Everyone was very proud of me for bringing a little happiness to Israel.' Go there, John! We're all Israeli now!

4. Noel Gallagher

He took drugs for England, he knocked the drugs on the head. And that was all we heard about the matter, for Noel was not one to wimp off to rehab, nor has he ever 'choked back the tears' about 'his drugs hell' in newspaper interviews. Most importantly, he has never hypocritically dissed anyone else who still canes it. It would be a sad day if everyone in the rock world gave up the sherbet, but if anyone could do it the right way, it was always going to be our Noel.

5. Irshad Manji

Just as there are any number of 'see-no-evil, speak-no-evil, hear-no-evil' non-Muslims who will refuse to accept that any bad is ever done in the name of Islam, so are there brave Muslims who can see only too well what is going on and just won't stop shouting about it, no matter who threatens them. Step forward and take a bow, Irshad Manji. Describing herself as a Muslim refusenik, she has spoken out eloquently about the excesses of Islamofascists and of her hope to change things for the better. Which is far more helpful than the 'I don't see what the problem is' modern hypocrites! Ms Manji is also a director of the Moral Courage Project in New York. Hmmm – 'moral' and 'courage' are two commodities in short supply in the lives of modern hypocrites.

THE HYPOCRITES' ULTIMATE WEEKEND

Ben and Siobhan are preparing for a special weekend they've been planning for the past four-and-a-half months. They've recently moved house – 'The most traumatic thing a human being can encounter, more so even than being a Muslim in modern Britain,' insists Siobhan – and so, although they normally believe that fun is for the young, they feel they have earned the right to let their hair down for once.

They previously lived in Brixton but moved house after finding they were no longer the only white *Guardian* readers clogging up the cafés on a Saturday morning. 'This place has lost its soul,' snapped Ben before frogmarching his wife to the nearest estate agents. So now they find themselves living in a housing association flat in Stoke Newington. It's great to be able to make a political statement just by where you live, so naturally they're very happy here.

Ben's daddy's money helps them make ends meet so all is well in their lives. The only drawback is the estate across the road from them: it really is an eyesore and Siobhan is sure that most of its inhabitants are racists, sponging off the state. No one could call Ben and Siobhan lazy: Ben works two days a week as an IT volunteer at an ethical investment company and Siobhan is a part-time healer.

They have two lovely children – Dylan and Evan – both of whom are highly gifted. Their au pair comes from the Sudan – she is a strong, proud woman. Before that there was the Bosnian, and the Croatian; funny how they always seem to come from places suffering from savage civil wars – must be their karma. Siobhan and Ben never think of au pairs as servants – they're part of the family! This being so, they don't want to complicate things with boring details like overtime pay and set-in-stone time off. And anyway, Ben isn't very good at negotiation or confrontation, so any time the au pair asks for a contract, he says: 'I'm just having some me time, can we talk about this later?'

It's Saturday afternoon and Ben and Siobhan are looking forward to a big night out. While Siobhan applies her Fairtrade make-up in the bedroom, Ben is in the lounge talking to his gay friend Colin on the phone. Ben isn't really listening to what his friend says, because he's also listening to his favourite hip-hop CD featuring a rapper chanting about raping bitches and burning gays to death. 'I'm so street,' thinks Ben.

They meet up with their friends Mohammad and Ayesha at an Ethiopian restaurant. Mohammad and Ayesha – who used to be Charlie and Emma – are recent converts to Islam and have brought gifts for Siobhan and Ben – keffiyeh scarves, which they proudly don, thus displaying their solidarity with the wholesome values of Islam. Ben suddenly remembers that white Emo girl he saw wearing a keffiyeh at the bus stop the day before and gets a guilty erection.

They eat Fairtrade goat curry, refuse to tip the waiter – he didn't even speak proper English! – and then it's off to the show, a revival of *My Name Is Rachel Corrie* at the Camden People's Theatre. After two hours of solid Israel-bashing, the quartet is in high spirits as they pile into an Irish pub for a 'cheeky half'. Ben has been badgering Ayesha for months to give up smoking, having kicked the habit last summer. However, so excited is he this evening that, when Ayesha pops out for a fag, he follows her and takes occasional puffs on her cigarette. (She smokes Camels; the packaging is so Middle

Eastern!) As some Muslims walk past, Ben says, 'Salem! Coming in for a real ale?' and is confused when they ignore him. To make up for it, he reminds Ayesha that he once did some work on lifeboats.

After the two couples say their farewells, Ben and Siobhan's mood is brought down somewhat on the night bus back when some nasty chavs insist on making noise on the top deck while they are trying to read the first edition of a Robert Fisk op-ed in the *Independent on Sunday*. (He's their hero; consider that time he was beaten up by those struggling Muslim boys and declared, 'I deserved it!') Siobhan suggests that Ben might ask them to pipe down. Ben refuses: 'I'm just trying to have some me time, OK?'

No sex for Ben tonight, then. As per! So while Siobhan is bathing, he swiftly downloads some 'barely legal' porn; since the birth of their first (much-wanted) child, he has effectively built up an immunity to milder sorts.

Meanwhile his wife is having a ylang-ylang 'Sensuality' bath with Neal's Yard oil and proving how sexually liberated she is by playing with the shower head. Back in front of the computer screen, Ben is mortified to ejaculate all over the T-shirt that he has had printed with his children's faces. It was made by Edun and very pricey but the firm is run by Bono's wife Ali, so buying it expressed both his solidarity and the solidity of his marriage. Together in bed, Ben kisses Siobhan goodnight and they go to sleep.

It's havoc in the morning when the 'mosque alarm clock' goes off and the kids wake up. Ben and Siobhan have awful hangovers; so much for that pricey organic wine, the grapes harvested while the moon was full so as not to make Mother Earth vexed! The au pair is off at the Lutheran church in Gresham Street, which she selfishly insists on doing every

Sunday; those Christian girls are just ME, ME, ME. Ben's going to have to have a word with her about this because, despite his planned conversion to Islam, he is hoping to get the kids into the local C. of E. school and will probably have to put in an appearance at the local church himself soon.

Ben and Siobhan get the kids together, swearing in Gaelic, and out of the house. They notice one of the families from the estate across the road is off on holiday. Ben waves them goodbye but secretly seethes at their irresponsible use of air travel. 'Why won't those chavs think about my children's future?' he says under his breath as he puts the key in the ignition of his 4 × 4 jeep.

So what to do on this sunny autumnal Sunday? So many choices! Ben and Siobhan don't know whether to take the kids to the local farmers' market – where you sign a pledge swearing that you won't ever eat a pig that wasn't born within three postcodes of your household – or to celebrate the joyous Muslim festival of Eid. They finally decide on a day at the allotment, acquired for a song from an old fireman moving to Essex – he was probably a racist, thinks Siobhan. The kids and Siobhan are bored within minutes of their arrival but Ben decides that 'on this occasion' he won't budge. 'After the week I've had I deserve some me time,' he whines.

So Siobhan takes the kids off to get a chai latte. On the way she stops to buy a copy of the *Big Issue* and is so horrified when the vendor asks if he can keep the change that she screams, 'The deal's off, give me back my money! Take your grubby little magazine and stick it up your greedy arse, you smelly little chav!'

As she sips her chai latte, Siobhan is forced to read a celeb mag that someone has left behind. Being a modern left-wing intellectual, she's horrified to see all the photographs of young white working-class women smiling and rolling out of bars in the early hours. Meanwhile, back at the allotment, Ben – who has just returned from a trip to the newsagent's – is in the shed, whacking one off over the exact same photographs.

Needing some groceries, Siobhan shouts, 'Fascists!' as she passes the local Tesco, and 'Jews ... I mean Zionists,' at M&S, going instead to a Fairtrade shop where she spends £29.99 on a pound of tomatoes and a loaf of rye bread. Handing over £30 in notes, she says generously, 'Keep the change, Abdul,' and drags the exhausted kids out of the store.

For Sunday afternoon, Ben is having more 'me time' when he goes to the local pub to watch the live Arsenal match. Ben has been a Gunners fan ever since they moved to the Emirates Stadium. 'Yes! Go, Super Reds, go!' he screams every time they get a throw-in. He misses the winning goal because he pops out for a fag, but he's still delighted that his favourite team beat Chelsea – he's always found it suspicious that Chelsea's Jewish owner appointed an Israeli manager. I mean, hello?! Not that he's anti-Semitic, merely anti-Zionist!

When he returns to the flat, he finds Siobhan reading *The Koran for Dummies* to their two comatose children. She used to prefer reading them Martin Amis novels because she loved how 'challenging and controversial' he was when he mocked white working-class people. But, when he criticised Islam, she burned all his books.

At the last moment, Ben decides to award their au pair a night off. She'd like to have had a bit of warning so she could have arranged something to do but she pretends to be delighted. And so it is that Ben and Siobhan end their perfect weekend by taking their au pair out for a slap-up meal at McDonald's (they want to treat her but don't want her getting too big for her boots, so they are putting on hold their deep opposition to fast-food chains for the night). 'I'm a nice guy, is all,' says Ben as he holds the front door open and lets the au pair and Siobhan walk in ahead of him.

'Oh well, back to work tomorrow,' says Siobhan as she kisses Ben goodnight. Ben turns over and a tear rolls down his cheek as he realises he has just had the greatest weekend of his life.

ACKNOWLEDGEMENTS

Julie would like to thank: Daniel Raven, Katie Glass, Edmund West and, most of all, Chas.

Chas would like to thank: Chris Morris, Katie Glass (she's mine), David J. Brown, Damian Schogger, Ashley Perry, Will Jessop, Tal Hevroni, Robert Caskie, Susi Weizman and – from the bottom of my heart – Julie.

INDEX